THE KILLING
OF WOLF
NUMBER TEN

THE KILLING OF WOLF NUMBER TEN

The True Story

THOMAS McNAMEE

PROSPECTA PRESS

Prospecta Press
P.O. Box 3131
Westport, CT 06880
www.prospectapress.com

Book and cover design by Barbara Aronica-Buck
Cover photograph by Barry O'Neill

"Northern Rocky Mountain Wolf Population Trends in Montana, Idaho and Wyoming: 1982–2012" chart on page 106 originally published in U.S. Fish and Wildlife Service, Rocky Mountain Wolf Recovery 2012 Interagency Annual Report.

"Sheep and Lamb Loss by Predators 2012" chart on page 108 originally published in United States Department of Agriculture, National Agricultural Statistics Service, Montana Sheep and Lamb Loss 2012.

Paperback ISBN: 978-1-63226-000-0
eBook ISBN: 978-1-63226-001-7

In memory of Wolves Nine and Ten

Nearly all of this book is based on action that I was present in or interviews that I have conducted. There are a few scenes that I have re-created from participants' recollections of them, and a few in which I have drawn inferences from scientific understanding of wolf behavior. Nothing has been invented. Within the limits of my ability, everything in this book is true.

– T.M.

I

January 12, 1995

A helicopter tops a line of spruce and skims the open snow. A man leans out, a gun at his shoulder, and then is lost from sight in a blur of swirling white and terrible noise.

The mother wolf and her daughter are running as fast as they can. The man shoots, a dart makes a hole in the snow, he shoots again and the dart sinks into the big wolf's thigh. The world slows down, grows quiet, grows vague, the light dies.

The small wolf sniffs at her mother's lips and open eyes, looks up in terror to see the helicopter returning, low above the snow, the roar unbearable.

There is a long, slow time until the blades droop and stop, and a man and a woman rush to the large black wolf. They tie a nylon mask over her eyes and wrap her gently in an old quilt, then do the same with the small pale wolf. The small wolf is wearing a radio collar. The man and woman carry the bundles across the snow and load them into the helicopter.

The mother wolf lies curled in a tight ball on a bed of straw inside a chain-link cage. She opens one eye to see her daughter in an adjacent cage. She looks out for only an instant. People are hurrying back and forth with metal things, cameras, medical bags, two-way radios, flashlights, lanterns. There are sounds of motors starting, cars and trucks leaving, the camp growing quiet. The sun goes down, a few electric lights come on.

A man approaches the cage, silent, holding a broomstick with a hypodermic needle taped to its tip. A quick jab and once again the black wolf's consciousness dims. Masked again, she is aware that people's hands are lifting her body and she should be afraid but she is not. They carry her on a stretcher to a corrugated metal building and lay her on a steel table. The lights are bright as summer noon, people are swarming over her, but their voices are soft. Mark Johnson, chief veterinarian of Yellowstone National Park, tells his assembled staff, "We've got to handle these wolves gently, respectfully, with love."

Network news videographers cluster around the medical tables, their white lights flaring. Reporters scratch at their pads, murmur into microphones. Flashes flash. It's a big story, the restoration of a race exterminated in its ancestral home seventy years ago.

The American biologists here, and the technicians, the officials of the United States Forest Service, Fish and Wildlife Service, National Park Service, all are holding their anxiety and fear at bay with a stiffened sense of duty and professionalism, which lends their voices a military brittleness:

"Body temperature 101, pulse 110, SpO2 ninety percent." (That last is oxygen saturation in the blood.)

"More straw for Pen Four, please."

"Right away."

"Fuel supply?"

"Adequate so far."

"Lights up, chopper incoming."

Equally if not more anxious and afraid, the conservationists who have come in their fragile confidence that this is really happening hug each other, trying not to celebrate too soon, knowing that at any moment, even now, all this can be shattered by a court order.

"What do you think they're up to?"

"God only knows."

The silence is what is so terrifying.

It is thirty below today in mid-Alberta, the sun a pale disc in a featureless sky, barely clearing the treetops at midday. Out from the

mountains in scraggy cut-over woodlands, a provincial park maintenance camp has been temporarily transformed into a nerve center,
dead center of concentric circles of worry and hatred hundreds and
thousands of miles across: Decades of struggle to return the wolf to
Yellowstone have culminated here.

The enemies of the wolf are legion and strong. Hatred of the wolf
is centuries old and needs no reason. Hatred drove the wolf to extinction throughout the lower forty-eight United States but for a tiny
remnant in Minnesota. The federal government itself exterminated
the wolves of Yellowstone. The last two were killed in 1926. For
twenty-five years the wolf's human friends have argued for restoration, and for twenty-five years the wolf's enemies have fought back
in the courts, in politics, and in the minds of ranchers and hunters
and anyone else who would listen.

At the dozens of hearings preceding the wolf reintroduction, there were always
demonstrations pro and con. This one was in Helena, Montana.

Many longtime residents of the northern Rocky Mountains believe
things about wolves that are not true. The ranching economy is fragile, and the hunting of big game in the untrammeled landscapes of

Wyoming, Idaho, and Montana is one of the last great freedoms left to a diminishing way of life. More than a few ranchers fear that wolves will kill enough calves to destroy all hope of profit. In a few cases they may be right. Many hunters think that wolves will reduce the elk and deer populations to miserable remnants. Occasionally, in combination with exceptionally brutal winters, wolves may reduce prey populations, but they never destroy them. The hunters' fears are wildly disproportionate. Some politicians have made of the wolf an all-purpose embodiment of evil, child killers even.

In fact wolves flee from any person. They kill cattle and sheep only seldom. And how could they destroy their prey populations? How could wolves, elk, bison, moose, and deer have evolved together down through the millennia? But hatred and fear, as the world has seen forever, can be impervious to truth.

The opposition has united behind the bland-sounding Wyoming Farm Bureau. All the recent years' high-horsepower lawyering wears that modest cloak. Only last week the U.S. Court of Appeals in Denver denied their plea for an injunction to block the wolf restoration. And now there's not a peep from them. Is it safe to believe they've given up at last?

At first she seemed black, but in this ice-blue light the dark wolf's fur can be seen to be silver-tipped, her undercoat gray, lighter gray, fawn. Human fingers search her coat and skin. "Some ticks. No open wounds. Moderate scarring."

"Oxymeter." A technician clips it to her lolling tongue. Her pulse, her respiration rate, her temperature, and the concentration of oxygen in her blood are all healthy. "Lice. Dust, please."

A second technician pulls back her black lip. "Teeth bright white, unchipped. Probably four years old." He measures every dimension of her body. "Ninety-eight pounds."

"Big for a girl."

"She's a good one."

The wolf's vulva is pink: She is in estrus, ready to breed.

No one knows where her mate may be, the alpha male of the

pack of which she is the alpha female. He evaded the traps that caught the black wolf and her daughter two months ago. That daughter, once collared and released, became what the biologists call a Judas wolf. She and her mother, thereafter, were easy to find. All the people here, and the dozens more elsewhere watching over every delicate step of this operation, would like to see that alpha male also caught, because it is the project's goal to capture whole families for Yellowstone—wolf packs are families). The plan has been to reintroduce three packs this year and three the next, in the hope that intact families will be less likely to try to return the thousand miles home to the north. But that older, wiser wolf has seen with his own eyes his mate and daughter trapped, and he is unlikely to be fooled now.

The technician draws a long dark draft of blood from the female wolf's foreleg, to be analyzed for rabies, parvovirus, and distemper. An earwax sample on a Q-tip goes into a test tube. Softly squeezing the wolf's lower belly, he pushes out a fecal sample, to be checked for parasites. He slides a fat pill of worm medicine down the wolf's throat. "Rabies, please." A first injection, then a second—"Penicillin, please"—to ward off any possible infection from all this poking by humans. "PIT tag, please." Through a shallow incision in the wolf's skin he inserts a Personal Identification Tag—essentially an invisible bar code, just like those available for pets—so that in future she (or her body) can be unmistakably identified.

He punches a plug of flesh out of each of the wolf's ears and slips them into a glass tube for DNA analysis. He clips a red plastic tag securely through each hole, bearing the letter Y, meaning that she is bound for Yellowstone, and the numeral 9.

All this has taken less than an hour. Number Nine reawakens on her bed of straw.

A Shorts Brothers Sherpa C-23—normally a fire-fighting plane, property of the U.S. Forest Service—sits in its hangar at Missoula, Montana, ready to take to the air and come here to Hinton, Alberta, to pick up the first group of wolves. There's a rumor that the Farm Bureau may be trying to come up with some last-second Hail-Mary move.

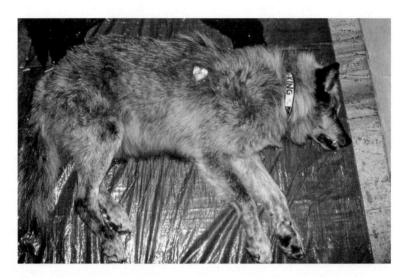

Wolf Number Thirteen, under anesthesia and ready for his medical exam at Hinton, January 1995. In a contest, a class of schoolchildren had given him the name King, but the professionals always used only the numbers. Some wolf watchers later called him Blue because of his unusual coloration.

"We don't have time to go for Nine's mate. We've got to get these wolves in the air."

"Helena's waiting to hear from Washington." That is, Ed Bangs, the head of the whole project for the U.S. Fish and Wildlife Service, based in Helena, Montana, is waiting to hear from Mollie Beattie, the director.

The conservationists are out of the loop now and can only speculate. But you can look at the agency people pacing up and down, the hard huffs of their breath in the icy air. You can listen to them not talking to each other. Waiting for the phone to ring. They more or less maintain their soldierly bearing, but everybody knows that most of them have devoted their careers and their hearts to this climactic moment.

"You think Mollie's waiting to hear from somebody higher up?"

"Who the hell knows."

"Let's go." The call has come. Mollie Beattie and her boss, Secretary of the Interior Bruce Babbitt, are ready to fly to Yellowstone for the most important event since its creation.

Mark Johnson, the Yellowstone vet, supervises the loading. After one last pre-flight medical check and a gentle dose of tranquilizer, each custom-made stainless steel shipping containers holds one baffled and disoriented but certified-healthy wolf. There are eight for Yellowstone National Park, and four for the parallel project to restore them to the wilderness of central Idaho. In Yellowstone there await three secure and hidden pens, in each of which, it is hoped, one family of wolves will gradually become accustomed to an entirely new environment. They will be set free only once they seem calm and ready. The Idaho wolves will be turned loose as soon as they arrive, to see if they will adapt as readily as some biologists believe to be possible. It is all an experiment, never tried before.

Everything is ready at Hinton. Then a call comes from Missoula. The runway has iced over, and the Sherpa cannot fly. Johnson decides that it will be less stressful to leave the wolves in their boxes. "They'll settle down." But he doesn't like it. Nobody does.

Then the ice melts, and the Sherpa takes off for Calgary. Then Calgary is socked in by fog and the plane flies on to Edmonton. At Edmonton the pilots find that their U.S. credit cards are not accepted by the Canadian phone system and so they cannot report back to Missoula or call the wolf team at Hinton. The weather toward Hinton in any case is "zero-zero"—zero ceiling, zero visibility. At long last, in mid-afternoon, which in these parts means dusk, the ceiling briefly parts, the Sherpa makes a break for it, and in the fading light the plane touches down.

Big, blond, rough-handed, tough-talking Carter Niemeyer believes this is the last he will see of these wolves. He has more to trap anyway, and had better do it quick. He has had his hands full getting this job done. It needed not just the best trapper—which he was—but also one who could deal with the isolated and suspicious trappers of backwoods Alberta. They were lucky to get four hundred dollars

Carter Niemeyer with the first Canadian wolf trapped for relocation.

for a good wolf pelt, and now this giant American shows up offering them *two thousand* for a *live* wolf? Smelled awful funny.

But Niemeyer has already seen a lifetime's share of ignorant and suspicious country boys. He has spent his whole career as an agent of the U.S. Department of Agriculture's Animal Damage Control unit— the on-purpose obscurely named outfit whose work consists almost entirely of killing animals that farmers and ranchers want killed. He has trapped and killed gophers, badgers, mountain lions, bears, and coyotes in the hundreds. He has even killed some wolves. But along the way, Niemeyer began to notice that some of the animals being blamed for depredations weren't guilty. Wolves had begun to recolonize Idaho and Montana from the north, and ranchers there were claiming a lot of wolf kills. When Niemeyer determined them to be otherwise, his bosses and colleagues still pressured him to find and kill wolves. He found himself more and more on the side of the persecuted predators. In his old gang's eyes, what Niemeyer is doing now—setting up and running a large-scale project to re-create two *extinct* wolf populations—is tantamount to treason. "Some of my bosses and contemporaries," he would write in his memoir, *Wolfer*, "would have been happy to see every predator in the West slung dead over a barbed-wire fence."

Mark Johnson seems as soft as Carter Niemeyer seems hard. Both those impressions on further examination will prove false, but they're the ideas they have of each other now. Johnson thinks Niemeyer's handling of the wolves is quite a bit on the rough side. "His excessive idealism got in my way," Niemeyer would write. "I didn't have the luxury of taking a wolf's pulse and temperature and putting an eyeshade on it when I had moments to get it out of a neck snare and make sure its airway was open."

He goes on to describe an exchange with Johnson when he, Niemeyer, is on the phone with a reporter who is also a friend of his. "Johnson began whispering that I should hang up, shut up. He made slashing motions at his throat.

"'Don't talk to reporters!' he said.

"'Just a minute, Arthur,' I said, smothering the receiver in my hand. 'Shut the fuck up and don't interrupt me when I'm on the phone!'"

Johnson remains acutely focused on the welfare of these wolves at this moment. His speech tends to be soft, there's nothing aggressive in his body language—in contrast to Niemeyer's pronounced swagger—but somehow he is always *here*, between the wolves and anything that might harm or frighten them: He is the one human being in this story who will be present in the wolves' lives throughout the whole operation, the one they will come to recognize as an individual with a particular touch, a particular voice.

With the last kennel lashed to the floor, Johnson belts himself in and the Sherpa climbs into the overcast, on a bearing for Calgary and Canadian customs. But once again Calgary is socked in, and the Sherpa tilts north toward Edmonton. Then the radio crackles, Calgary has opened up. Johnson is as still and silent as his wolves, and equally resigned. They slip into Calgary under lowering clouds, and the Canadian customs officials rush them through, and soon they're airborne again, this time for Great Falls, Montana, and United States customs, whence they are to fly on to Missoula. There they will meet a caravan of vehicles manned by park and forest rangers and be driven the last three hundred miles to Yellowstone.

Johnson oversees the unloading of the wolves to a heated hangar at the Great Falls airport and goes through the paperwork with the customs officers. Meanwhile he's hearing yelling from inside the crew lounge—the pilots on the phone with their boss. It seems they've hit the limit of their statutorily allowed flying hours, and no, they will not be granted a single hour's extension, which is all they need to get to Missoula. The caravan, still somewhere on the road, does have a cell phone, but nobody has the number. Johnson covers his mouth with both hands, then goes back to check on the wolves. In some of the ventilation slots there is fresh blood: The wolves have begun to try to chew their way out.

Johnson calls his colleagues, knowing that there's nothing to be gained. The tranquilizers have long since worn off. The wolves have been handled with all the tenderness their handlers could muster, but think about it: Darted, drugged, blindfolded, poked, prodded, caged, boxed up, trucked, loaded, pitching and yawing for hours inside this noise machine, unloaded, reloaded, bombarded by the voices and noises and smells of their one great source of terror—humanity—the wolves are under inconceivable stress. It is not unusual for wild animals in the stress of no more than ordinary captivity just to drop dead. These wolves' lives may be at stake.

Eventually the rangers reach Missoula and learn that they must drive on to Great Falls. At three o'clock in the morning, they arrive. The crew load the four wolves for Idaho onto a truck, and then the other eight into a long horse trailer. Mark Johnson follows them into the trailer, craving sleep, unable to find it even after twenty-four hours awake. Inside their carriers, the wolves lie still, eyes closed, withdrawn, beyond exhaustion.

It is dank cold and still dark as the caravan sets forth for Yellowstone. Patrol cars front and rear and several large National Park Service SUVs provide security. The rangers are packing serious armament, for anywhere along the way there could easily be some crank who would love to put a hole in a wolf, or for that matter in a wolf-loving G-man.

The wolf returns to Yellowstone in glory. Schoolchildren cheer and wave American flags. Camera lenses glitter in the morning sun in hundreds. Television news teams have descended on the national park from around the world, their logo-emblazoned vans tilting their dishes toward their relay satellites. Video crews are shooting video of other video crews. Part of the coverage is how much coverage there is.

Half a dozen just-polished ranger patrol cars flashing red and blue and, behind them, a long gray horse trailer containing eight wolves and their vigilant veterinarian drive slowly through the little town of Gardiner, Montana, in a surge of cheers. At the horizon looms the Roosevelt Arch, which commemorates the creation of the world's first national park in 1872. The motorcade passes beneath it at eight thirty-five a.m., to the blare of band music and the roar of the hundreds gathered to welcome them. With a stop at park headquarters,

On January 12, 1995, the gray wolf returned to Yellowstone. From left to right, project leader Mike Phillips, park maintenance foreman Jim Evanoff, U.S. Fish and Wildlife Service director Mollie Beattie, Yellowstone Park superintendant Mike Finley, and Secretary of the Interior Bruce Babbitt brought the first of the wolves in its shipping kennel to the Crystal Creek pen.

the big brass join the parade: the park superintendent, Mike Finley; the director of the U.S. Fish and Wildlife Service, Mollie Beattie; and the Secretary of the Interior, Bruce Babbitt. Following them come park service senior staff and the park's own team of biologists, who will be taking charge of the wolves now.

Past this point, the park is closed to all but these few and a press pool. In solitude, therefore, the caravan makes its processional way some twenty miles to the south and east, to the lower valley of the Lamar River, where the last wolves of Yellowstone perished, in 1926, and where these eight wolves and another group soon to come are now to make their new homes.

The Lamar and the rolling grassland savannas below its confluence with the Yellowstone River constitute what is known as the Northern Range. It is one of the world's great places for wildlife, comparable in richness to the Serengeti Plain of east Africa. The Northern Range this winter is home to perhaps eighteen thousand elk, about two thousand mule deer, five hundred bighorn sheep, several hundred antelope, two hundred moose, a few white-tailed deer, a few mountain goats, and five or six hundred descendants of the last wild bison left alive in the United States in the eighteen-eighties. In summer, most of those numbers roughly double. There are seven other herds of elk besides the huge Northern Herd. The wolves will have enough to eat.

The snow here at six thousand two hundred feet is about a foot deep, the wind raw as a whip. A truck-sized sleigh drawn by two sly-looking mules waits at the trailhead. On the rough board seat sit two impressively bearded mule drivers. Two wolf containers are lashed to the bed, and the sleigh lurches forward. It moves slowly up the narrow drainage of Rose Creek, to a sparsely forested hollow of aspen and lodgepole pine in which there stands a roughly round chain-link

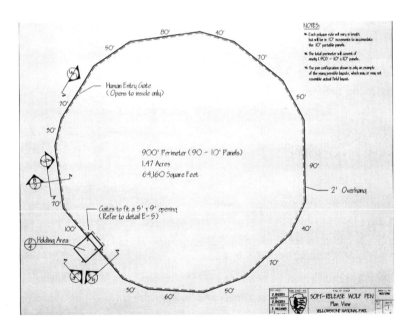

The actual pens varied somewhat from this idealized schematic, having to conform to their individual sites' topography and to be situated so that they were invisible from any road.

enclosure, one acre in size. The fence is ten feet tall with a further inward-slanting two feet of chain link at the top and an apron of chain link beneath the soil extending inward three feet—designed so that the wolves can neither climb out nor dig out. The pen cannot be seen from the road. The wolves will see as little of humanity as possible—only the biologists who will come to drop off road-killed elk or deer from time to time. Hidden from the wolves and from possible intruders, armed park rangers will be guarding them twenty-four hours a day.

The gate is open. Inside is little but open space—a few trees, a doghouse where a wolf feeling shy may hide. Strong hands gently lower the kennels to the ground and carry them into the pen. Wolf Number Nine and her daughter, now designated Seven, are in their new home. The other six wolves, an intact pack, are delivered to the pen at Crystal Creek, a few miles away, with Babbitt and Beattie carrying them the last few dozen yards and smiling officially for the cameras. Automated shutters click and whir, tape rolls, the pool reporters scribble. It is a media moment par excellence, as the evening news tonight and the front-page photographs across the country tomorrow morning will attest.

But it's all a sham, a tragic, idiotic sham.

The jubilation at the entrance to the park, the flag-waving children, the brass bands, the satellite dishes, the whole parade have been in vain, for the order sought by the Farm Bureau and the anti-wolf groups sheltering under its name has come from the Tenth Circuit Court in Denver—an emergency stay of forty-eight hours. The kennels may be placed inside the acclimation pens, but they may not be opened. The return of the wolf to Yellowstone is on hold.

Nine and Seven have no idea where they are, of course. They have been jounced, shaken, pitched, and rattled for untold hours inside metal boxes with only small holes for air. The noises have been loud, harsh, and utterly foreign. Now at last it is quiet, but still they lie inside their steel cells.

Mark Johnson pushes chunks of ice through the holes, which the thirsty wolves lick up eagerly. He wishes he could speak soft words to them, but he also knows that the less they have of any human presence, the better off they will be in the future.

If they have a future. The judges may rule that the wolves must be returned to Canada, but the Canadians have already said they won't take them—in which case they must be euthanized.

At seven-thirty that morning Alice Thurston of the U.S. Department of Justice was already in court in Denver arguing, *please*, the wolves can be let out of the kennels and into the pens without actually being *released*. Then at least they can have water, and light, and food. They can stretch their miserably cramped legs. And if the court so orders they can easily be rounded up. But the judges will have none of it.

Mark Johnson tells his colleagues at park headquarters that the wolves' condition is bad. If this situation continues, he says, it could be fatal.

Federal officialdom makes its stand before the cameras, each personage going on a little longer than strictly necessary for sound-bite usage.

Yellowstone Park superintendent Mike Finley: " . . . Injustice. . . ."

Secretary of the Interior Bruce Babbitt: " . . . Extraordinary moment in the history of the American West . . . who we are in America. . . ."

Fish and Wildlife Service director Mollie Beattie: "This is going to be wolf heaven if we can just get them out of purgatory."

The biologists gather in uneasy silence, nothing to say.

Yellowstone wolf project leader Mike Phillips takes a seat at the end of the big table in the park's executive conference room and hunches at a taped-up cluster of microphones. Phillips is blond, compact, tense as a drawn bow. The straight set of his lips indicates the pressure of his passion contained—passionate anger. Having led the restoration of red wolves to North Carolina, Phillips has considerable experience with wolf controversy. His experience has not made him patient, however.

Thanks to the dirty pool played by the reintroduction's opponents, the wolves were confined to their shipping containers for thirty-eight hours. This is Number Seven, Number Nine's daughter.

The room is stinking hot, and jammed. Flashes and spotlights blind and irritate. Unkempt print reporters scribble on their little pads. The wolf reintroduction is the biggest story Yellowstone has ever had.

Phillips squints into the TV lights. "These wolves have been in their kennels for thirty hours straight. When wolves are extremely stressed," he says—very slowly—"they have a tendency to slip into a stupor of sorts. These wolves have done that. They are not doing well." He does not say, "They may die," but that is what he means.

This court order was really a punch below the belt. The Farm Bureau could have filed its appeal much earlier, but they timed it so that if they succeeded the wolves would be already on the way. They wanted to inflict the maximum damage possible, and they have done it.

In uncanny complement to Mike Phillips's dense muscularity, Yellowstone's chief wolf biologist, Doug Smith, has the stretched, lean boniness of a movie cowboy, complete with mustache and reserve.

But he is no less tightly wound today. He visits the pens repeatedly, opens the doors of the kennels to find the wolves cowering and still, making no move to rise, much less to leave. Having worked for years on the great decades-long Isle Royale study, Smith knows wolves well and up close, and he knows how bad these wolves look. Back at park headquarters at Mammoth Hot Springs, he speaks one sentence: "This is sickening."

The afternoon wears on. No one goes home. Justice is begging the court—please, please to hurry their decision. At seven o'clock in the evening the phone rings. The stay is lifted.

There is no need for Mike Phillips to say more than "Let's go." He and Doug Smith and the rest of the wolf crew jump into their trucks and blaze along the ice-covered roads to the pens. They draw up the vertically sliding kennel doors and secure them, quietly lock

When the shipping containers were finally opened, the wolves were beyond exhaustion.

the pen gates, and withdraw in a hurry. By the time all the wolves' boxes have been opened, it is ten-thirty p.m. The wolves have been caged for thirty-eight hours. And yet, at Crystal Creek, not one of the six wolves will leave its kennel. Nor, at Rose Creek, will Nine. Seven, however, puts a cautious foot to the snow, sniffs the chill night air, and steps forth into Yellowstone.

Hours later, her mother stands at last and, wobbily, walks out into the night. There is snow to eat, to quench their thirst. There is a big haunch of elk.

In a brief celebration at the wolf project office back at park head-quarters, there are quick beers of relief, then in blurred succession fol-low shallow sleep, gathering in the frozen dark of five in the morning, coffee in the truck, and finally lying belly down in the snow behind a low ridge above the pen with spotting scopes until first light.

By dawn Nine and Seven have eaten most of their haunch of elk, and have sniffed and scent-marked the pen's whole perimeter. At mid-morning they are running, running, running, mouths agape, tongues hanging out, silent, around and around, just inside the fence, pound-ing a dark path in the snow.

Back in Alberta, Carter Niemeyer and his crew keep trapping. Within a week they have eleven more wolves for Idaho and six for Yellowstone. Among the latter is one extraordinary light-buff male, very big—a hundred and twenty-two pounds—and possessed of an imposing bearing. There is about this wolf a calm, a quiet, a confi-dence, something magisterial, something none of these people long familiar with wolves have seen quite the equal of before. Unlike any of the other wolves, he will stare you straight in the eye and keep star-ing. He has bitten two jab sticks in half. He has the big balls of a breeder. Everyone agrees: Number Ten, as he will henceforth be known, is the very definition of an alpha male. He will make the per-fect mate for Number Nine.

—If they don't kill each other first. Unrelated wolves, when entirely strangers, and especially in close quarters, may well fight to

Muleteer Ben Cunningham and his indefatigable Billy took food to the wolves on a sleigh—in fair weather and foul.

the death. That is why the wolf team wanted so badly to capture intact families. The hope now is that Nine's advanced state of estrus will overcome whatever hostility might arise between her and this magnificent alpha male.

Even after his trapping and his several anesthetizations, his medical exams, all that handling by people, his long trip to Yellowstone in a stainless steel cage, Number Ten, unlike any of his predecessors, seems neither disoriented nor exhausted. He does not cower in his kennel. When the biologists slide the door open, he strides right out and goes straight to Number Nine. Young Seven edges cautiously away from what she instantly recognizes as grown-ups' business. Ten gives Nine a thorough stem-to-stern sniffing. She stands for it with a sort of frozen dignity and, in due course, a certain amount of reserved reciprocal sniffing.

Ten lays his head across the back of Nine's neck. This is not a romantic gesture. In wolf language it means, I like you, yes, but I also outrank you. Nine bridles, snarls, and scoots out from beneath Ten's embarrassed expression of tough love.

Nine and Ten stiffen and stand tall, growling. They come together slowly, touch noses, sniff each other's rears, snarl, and separate. Two hours of nastiness pass, but they have not fought. By the end of the day, each has occupied the farthest possible reach of the pen from the other. From time to time one or the other will open an eye and mutter a low growl.

By next morning, Nine and Ten are curled up together, by no means with the easy slump of puppies but nonetheless together, and asleep.

There is about this wolf a calm, a quiet, a confidence, something magisterial . . .

. . . the very definition of an alpha male.

II

No photograph does better justice to Nine's sheer vitality than this one.

January 30, 1995

The idea of the acclimation pens is to hold the wolves in place while they become accustomed to the sights and, most importantly, the smells, of Yellowstone. The canine world is a universe of scent. The wolf's olfactory acuity is something we can barely imagine. Scent marking is the wolf's primary medium of communication. Wolves find their way with their noses, recognize one another by smell, and by scent know danger—they know the world by its aromas.

Surely, then, they haven't been fooled into thinking that the Lamar River valley is anything like Alberta. To start with, their home smelled always of wolves: It was a quilt of occupied territories, one

Ten and Nine often circled the pen together.

Nine's daughter, who accompanied her from Canada, Number Seven.

Seven shared her mother's inexhaustible vitality.

pack to each, each with a boundary constantly patrolled and scent-marked with little squirts of urine and rubbings of glandular secretions, here a tree, there a rock, each scent mark rich with meaning. The last time Yellowstone was quilted with wolf territories and its air dense with their scent was more than a century ago. What Nine, Ten, and Seven smell now is the absence of wolves.

Yet wolf presences are making themselves known a little more every day. The other two pens are not far away, and when the wind is right, surely all the wolves scent their co-detainees. In the right wind, or none, they hear one another's howls. But they know they are *not at home*, and that is the Yellowstone wolf team's great worry—that no matter how long they are confined, that no matter how well they come to understand the wealth of prey that awaits them in the Lamar, when at last the gates of the pens are opened, the wolves will go home.

Wolves have been known to run for hundreds of miles. They have an uncanny sense of direction. Domestic dogs—their descendants, and quite similar in their sensory apparatus—have found their way home innumerable times, across highways, railroads, golf courses, Walmart parking lots. The acclimation pens are an experiment. This has never been done before.

Number Nine's coat sometimes looked black, but it was really multicolored.

Number Ten feeding on road-killed elk in the Rose Creek pen.

In January 1995, while Carter Niemeyer and his troops were trapping wolves in Alberta, a new United States Congress was taking its seat in Washington, D.C. Both houses are now controlled by Republicans. Newt Gingrich is Speaker of the House, and newly elected members from the far right are joining long-established opponents of the wolf reintroduction in crafting legislation to end it. New lawsuits are brewing as well.

Mike Phillips, Doug Smith, and all their web of support—not only the Fish and Wildlife Service and the National Park Service and the deeply engaged Secretary of the Interior but also wolf biologists, wolf devotees, ecologists, and thousands of conservationists around the world—are watching Yellowstone with riveted attention. This is the moment when the whole thing really could collapse.

Here is the dilemma the decision makers are facing. On one hand, you want to keep the wolves in the pens as long as possible, for acclimation's sake. On the other hand, that also means that in the event of either a legislative or a court victory by the anti-wolf forces, the argument that the Justice Department employed to try to help the wolves can now be turned against them: In a one-acre-pen, it's easy to dart a wolf. With no export option, euthanasia would be the next step. The End.

Here is why the return of the wolf to Yellowstone matters so much. Besides being the world's first and most famous national park, Yellowstone is also the heart of the Greater Yellowstone Ecosystem— the largest remaining essentially intact ecosystem in the temperate zones of the earth. And the single element missing from the ecosystem's completeness is its top predator. The loss of top predators worldwide has been one of conservation's saddest failures. Without their top predators, ecosystems begin to unravel.

The whole history of conservation has been—the very word says it—about saving things. Here is an opportunity to show, on a heroic scale, that humankind can begin to *heal* the damage it has inflicted on the earth, not just to rescue something nearly lost but to restore something altogether lost. This experiment, if it should succeed, will

Nine and her daughter Seven in the Rose Creek Pen.

be one of the greatest conservation victories in history. It is already the most dramatic event in Yellowstone's history.

The wolf team can't stop talking.

"I say we open the gates now, we take the chance. Sure, they may head north toward home, and that'll be failure of the experiment. It doesn't mean we can't try again."

"Are you kidding? This is our one shot."

"And maybe they'll stay. Maybe the acclimation has worked. "

"Yeah, and let's say then the court orders us to round them up. What then?"

"After what they've been through?"

"Exactly. They'd be almost impossible to trap."

"They could shoot them from the air."

"They could. But not with my help."

"Mine neither."

"They could get one of Carter's old buddies. They'll kill anything."

"But think about this. By the time they got through the appeals and all, the collars' batteries would all be dead."

"I'll drink to that."

"So we're agreed?"

"Hell yes."

"Open 'em up!"

Now word comes that one Idaho wolf has done all the others one big non-favor. He has killed a newborn calf. Much has been made by wolf advocates of how unlikely it will be that wolves will kill livestock in areas of abundant wild prey. This calf lived (and died) in a virtual sea of elk and deer. The wolf biologists have known all along that this was bound to happen, the environmentalists knew it too, they all just sort of played it down—and hoped it might happen not quite so soon.

Mike Phillips insists the Fish and Wildlife Service investigators are pretty sure that the calf died of natural causes, shortly after its birth—and lab tests will later confirm that—but it's too late for mere facts.

A good example of how dangerous wolves are. Doug Smith is capturing Number Three, an eighty-pound male from the Crystal Creek pack, with a salmon net.

Three is caught. His wide-open mouth is not an expression of menace but rather one of fear.

Number Three really did want to get out, of course, and luckily Mike Phillips was there with a second net.

Once subdued, Three got an injection of tranquilizer and a medical examination. Here Deb Guernsey and Mike Phillips are waiting for the drug to wear off before releasing him.

And so. The wolf-haters chalk up another point on the scoreboard, and yet another hearing is scheduled in Washington. There's no time to waste. The Yellowstone wolf team know they've got to get those wolves out of the pens and on the ground, come what may.

March 21, 1995

The sun of this first day of spring is headache-bright on wide white meadows crosshatched with animal footprints. Snow-dust wind-wracked from the Douglas-firs on the mountainsides swirls into snow-devils on the flat, dervishing down to the frozen Lamar River. Bison nest in pits in the snow. A few cud-chewing elk lie bedded just inside the forest edge. The south-facing slopes, melting bare, have been nibbled and trampled into barely vegetated mud by the thousands of elk that winter in this valley.

A few first faint washes of green have appeared on the sunniest prominences. A thin cloud settles on the summit of a black mountain called The Thunderer. Mountain goats live up there, in inconceivable weather. Dozens of mountain bluebirds, still in their migration flocks, flutter across the valley floor.

At four forty-five in the afternoon, a crew of biologists, the one allowed reporter, and a videographer hike through deep snow up over Crystal Bench and down to the pen containing the Crystal Creek pack. Mike Phillips unlocks the gate.

The wolves flee to the farthest reach of the pen, pacing fretfully back and forth in the black mud they have churned up there. Twice a week for ten weeks, people have come to leave the elk, deer, and bison carcasses that have sustained the wolves through their incarceration, and every human visit has been marked by this anxiety and stymied flight. Familiarity has not tamed these wolves.

Working quickly, the men set up the electronic motion detectors that are to alert them by radio when the wolves pass through the gate

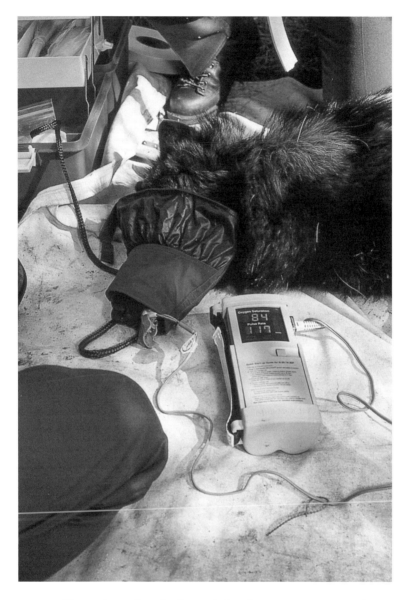

Every wolf got a thorough medical exam before the pen gates were opened.

Doug Smith had to get used to hoisting the hundred-pound dead weight of a tranquilized wolf.

and into the world. The videographer aligns and focuses a camera that will run unattended for the next two hours to record for posterity the Crystal Creek pack's first free steps in Yellowstone.

The crew leave eight pounds of road-killed elk inside the pen, another thirty pounds ten yards outside. The wolves haven't been fed for four days. Their bellies are empty.

Back at the trailhead, cigars are distributed. Puffs of triumph rise stinking into the breeze and evanesce.

One big "Yee-*ha!*" and a group high-five are all the celebration necessary.

As the sun descends, the Lamar awakens. Eleven bull elk, still splendidly antlered though soon to doff their crowns, appear on a ridgeline, then twenty-six, soon a hundred and more, all bulls. A herd of cow elk and their calves—at least a hundred of each—move out of the trees and down to the roadside where sun-warmed asphalt and snowmelt have greened a fringe of grass.

Ravens, winter's old familiars, call *rock-rock* in the lodgepoles. Two Brewer's blackbirds natter in a cottonwood top. A golden eagle walks along a snow-crusted hillside, rolling at the shoulders like a bar bully. A family of coyotes set up a boisterous yipping somewhere to the north, behind one of the few healthy aspen groves left in this elk-gnawed valley. Will wolf predation bring back the aspen the elk have suppressed? In time we will see—that is, if the wolves will stay here.

There are elk everywhere. Quite a few are in bad shape at this time of year, after a typically brutal Yellowstone winter and when their food supply is at its annual nadir. Some are already dead, lying crumpled downwind from a lee of drift. This is a good place to be a wolf.

Wolf Number Ten.

Phillips and Smith drive the valley until one in the morning, alternating who wears the headphones, listening for the first radio signal to announce the freedom of wolves in Yellowstone. Nothing. At six a.m. the Crystal Creek pack remain resolutely inside their pen.

March 22

Once again Mike Phillips faces cameras and reporters in the over-heated park conference room. Phillips tends to look younger than his actual thirty-six. This morning he is distinctly gray. After years of defending his North Carolina wolf project against absurd misunderstandings, Phillips is a practiced spinmeister, but his passion to be clearly understood tends to emerge in an oddly argumentative tone, as though he is countering an accusation. Indeed the whole truth—what the reporters cannot know—is that he is arguing with himself.

THE KILLING OF WOLF NUMBER TEN   37

"This is perfect, perfect," he insists. "We wanted them to come out on their own terms. We just have to be patient.

"There are two possible explanations" for the wolves' refusal to budge, he says. One is simple wariness of human scent. "Wolves in Alberta are trapped, snared, and shot year-round. In fact, to keep a trapping license in Alberta you have to show that you have killed some certain *minimum* number of wolves annually, and there is no maximum limit. Human-caused wolf mortality in the Hinton region approaches forty percent per year." From an Alberta wolf's point of view, anything that smells like people could be final trouble.

"Since the gate of the pen is precisely the place they associate with human intrusion," he explains, "it would be perfectly natural for these wolves to be extremely cautious about a change of circumstance there."

Everybody has been careful to stay as short a time as possible when they bring the carcasses, and observations of the packs have not only been rare, they've been conducted from long distances. Wolves are just naturally terrified of people. A wolf pack that will rip a nine-hundred-pound elk's throat out without flinching will run like hell at the first scent or sight of a sixty-pound child.

Sometimes it would take the wolves an hour to calm down after a visit by the feeders, Phillips explains. The paths they have worn in all three pens all veer wide of the gates: The wolves have avoided people-places even when no people were present.

"The second possible explanation," he continues, "is that the wolves may have no concept of an opened gate as something you can just walk through, any more than they had had a concept of chain-link fence. In their first days in the pens, the wolves crashed into the fences, they tried to dig under them, and they bloodied their muzzles trying to figure out just what this thing was that was keeping them in. They may not even *know* that they've been set free now."

"The fact of the matter," says Phillips, "is that the Crystal Creek pack has already begun to allay everybody's worst fear, that they would streak the thousand miles straight home to Canada. We don't even know if they're going to remain a pack." Family life is the foundation

of wolf nature, but stress is often reflected in changes in pack struc-
ture—alphas deposed, subordinates kicked out, new wolves joining,
fights, sometimes even murder.

"Nobody really knows how much stress these wolves have been
feeling." After the first few frantic days in the pens, the wolves did
seem to settle down. They ate, from the beginning, like wolves. They
have not fought. "The packs have howled often, which wolves in dis-
tress do not do. The best indication that they're feeling all right is that
all three alpha pairs have been seen mating."

But when you get right down to it—Phillips does not say this—
no one has the faintest idea of what's going on.

March 23

Nine and Ten are mates now. She can feel the stirring in her belly.
Ten howls and howls. There is always plenty to eat in the pen, but he
sees and smells elk on the hoof, and his hunting instinct is burning
inside him.

When people bring food to the pens, every other wolf but one
runs away. Each pen has a sort of doghouse shelter, and the shyest
wolves dive into those or cower behind them. Only Number Ten is
not afraid. While Nine and Seven modestly seek the pen's far edge,
Ten dodges behind his keepers as if to tease them, and then will race
around the pen perimeter. The way his tongue lolls out and his eyes
glitter, it's almost as though he's laughing. The minute they leave,
Wolf Number Ten hops on top of his house for a better view of their
good riddance, and often a nice loud howl too.

The Crystal Creek pack having made no move to go anywhere
for three days and nights, the biologists open the gate of the Rose
Creek pen. Nine, Ten, and Seven trot nervously back and forth,
watching the people's every move. Surely big brave Ten will lead his
family to freedom. But no. All night, the sensors are silent. The Roses

There seemed to be no end to Number Ten's energy.

It turned out to be a good thing that so many deer and elk are dumbstruck in headlight beams. The penned-in wolves lived on roadkill.

won't go near the open gate.

On the thesis that the stink of humanity has poxed the Crystals' gate, the wolf team cut a hole in that pen's wall at the back and tie down the carcasses of two deer outside.

The wolves watch, uneasy. When the people are gone, they cluster in silence, sniffing at one another and whimpering softly. The deer smell good, and they're hungry, but every one of them knows from experience that meat that has been touched by a person could well be concealing a steel-jawed trap or, worse, a neck snare, to either of which the only consequence is either freezing to death or a bullet to the brain. A number of these wolves have seen an uncle, an aunt, a father, a mother, a sister, a brother, make that very mistake. Others, when young and naïve, were simply punished by an elder for going too near. In any case all of them know that this looks like a dangerous situation, quite possibly a trick, yet as their hunger deepens all of them also are tempted.

The coyote packs are howling day and night—five times more than usual, a researcher reports. Wolves hate coyotes, and will kill them whenever they can. Not for food—no one really knows why. Coyotes fear wolves with good reason. Sometimes when the coyotes howl, the wolves growl and bark. They all know change is imminent.

Paul Harvey, the right-wingish radio pundit, reflecting that the wolves have been so well fed by the government that they must just want to stay on the dole, has been half-joking about "welfare wolves."

The biologists are perplexed. One of their sensors has told them that something has gone *into* the Rose Creek pen. They do not yet know that the sensor was—oops—installed backward, and that what it is saying is that Ten has departed.

March 24

"Unit one, message oh-one," the radio squawks at 9:04 a.m. This is an automated signal from the motion detectors at the newly cut hole in the Crystal Bench pen. Whenever those sensors fire, they are then inactive for five seconds. Therefore this signal may mean one wolf, two, three, four, five, or six if they moved fast. It may also mean a windfall chute of snow from a tree.

"Unit one, message oh-one," it says again at 10:17, again at 10:24, 10:29, 10:30, 10:35. This is not snow. This is a pack of six wolves.

Here's what has happened. Two rash yearlings could contain themselves no longer. Bellies to the snow, they slunk to the deer and ripped out great chunks, gobbling them down so fast they nearly choked and then dashing back to the safety of the pen. Seeing that they survived this foolish adventure, their packmates have been sneaking out to feast on the deer and then, with the first rustle of breeze or crack of twig, losing their nerve.

Unlike all the other wolves, Ten was never afraid to look a person in the eye.

Late afternoon, the crew head up Rose Creek to cut a hole for Nine, Ten, and Seven at the heavily trampled area that is obviously their comfort zone. They are also going to leave a fresh deer carcass just outside. Snow is falling heavily. They are only partway to the pen when from behind and above them comes a long, low howl.

About a hundred yards away, silhouetted on the ridgeline in the swirling snow and mist, stands Number Ten, looking straight at them and howling without letup. This is *my* mountain.

They drop the deer and hightail it down to the road, exulting. Wolf Number Ten is free in Yellowstone.

March 25

Now is the critical moment: Will the wolves start for home? As tempting as it may be to try to get a look at them, the biologists believe that the slightest disturbance could set them fleeing, and so they stay away. The Crystal Creek pack have made a couple of heroic forays, the first a quarter-mile, the second two whole miles to Specimen Ridge, a vantage point from which they could survey the sweeping length and breadth of the lower Lamar—but they keep returning to their pen.

Ten continues restlessly circling the Rose Creek pen, but Nine and Seven remain inside. The Soda Butte pen will stay locked up until what these first wolves do seems more or less certain.

March 26

Nine has still not taken a single step outside. Ten is circling and circling, howling and howling, and Nine, in response, grows more and more agitated. She is pregnant. She feels the ancient urge to dig a den and hide herself away to give birth, but she knows that this is not the place to do it. Yet she is afraid to leave. The world out there is not her home. Is Ten telling Nine that they can still try to make it home? Does he, somehow, know the way? Whatever sense of trust Nine may once have had—and through generations of selection for mistrust in Alberta it may have been scant—her sense of trust now is fragile indeed.

March 27

L. David Mech, by general agreement America's leading authority on the gray wolf, has flown in. John Varley, the head of scientific research for Yellowstone National Park, calls Dave Mech "the alpha of alphas," but as seems so often the case in leaders of real stature, Mech (pronounced "meetch") does not fit a simple set of dominance criteria. His appearance is unprepossessing. He is drably dressed, bald, bearded, tall but a little stooped, quick-moving, tightly wound but also calm, with dark, penetrating eyes behind hooded lids. Sometimes he seems a little breathless, scattered, distracted. The impression of distraction is misleading, however, for he has a quality of constant and intense attention that is more like a wild animal's than that of other human beings. He is lean, soft-spoken, aware, *attuned*—like a wolf. Like a wolf, he is a watcher and a listener. When he sees you, you know you have been recognized, and when he listens, you know you have been heard.

Dave Mech, "the alpha of alphas" of wolf science.

Mech has worked in close consultation with everybody on this project for years, and hardly a whit of its design and execution has come to pass without his approval. Much of it, in fact, derives from Mech's decades of field research in Minnesota, in Alaska, and in the famous wolf-moose study on Isle Royale in Lake Superior. When the first informal discussions of a Yellowstone reintroduction began percolating thirty years ago, it was Mech whom the Park Service called on to appraise the feasibility of the idea. His authority is unquestioned.

Doug Smith, the number two Yellowstone wolf biologist, who will inherit the project when Mike Phillips moves on, studied under Mech at Isle Royale and shares with him an air of modest reticence— false in both cases.

Phillips is the always the boldest presence in the discussion, and sometimes gives an opposite impression, of all broadcast no receive, but that would be a false conclusion as well. A good new idea stops him in his tracks.

A gang of biologists are gathered in the lee of a big glacial boulder in the Lamar playing a ferocious game of spades, with bellows of victory and groans of defeat interspersed with serious discussion about the problem they're facing.

"I think it's just the human scent on the gates, simple as that," says Smith.

"Agree, as far as it goes," says Phillips. "But suppose they just don't have the mental image that we do of an 'opening.'"

Steve Fritts, of the Fish and Wildlife Service, says, "Think how unfamiliar everything they see is. Humans foresee the whole sequence—capture, transport, acclimation, release—and we assume, Well, they *must* want freedom. But the human idea of freedom may not be the wolf idea. We can't know what their experience is."

"I think we need to cut a hole in the fence right in the middle of their safety zone," says Phillips.

"What about at the far end of the pen?" counters Smith.

"Well, in the future maybe we ought to have automated doors, so nobody ever touches them."

"Change the shape of the pens."

"Have you been thinking about how close together these pens are? And what might happen when they finally do come out? I'm worried about conflict between the packs."

"That's why we want to let them all out at the same time, so no one pack can establish a territory and defend it."

Mech speaks for the first time in a while: "We've seen pack density at that level. Or they could just spread out, you know."

"It still worries me," says Smith.

"Yeah," says Phillips, "let's find more things to worry about."

Mech says quietly that he really doesn't know what to do now, but he does have an idea, only an idea.

Everyone listens.

The Soda Butte pen is the only one that hasn't been opened,

right? So we've got a fresh opportunity there. Suppose we not even bother opening the gate—just remove a great wide section of the fence at the opposite end of the pen. As far as possible from the slightest trace of human scent. And not a gate that they have to find their way through, a whole big open space where what's held them in has just disappeared.

Unanimous agreement. This is why you call on Dave Mech.

March 28

The Sodas have also not been fed for more than a week, and now the biologists plant a deer and a half just outside the pen, just beyond the movement sensors. After a whole afternoon of staring longingly at the meat, in the fading light of evening two of the Sodas skulk outside to rip into it, and later that night the others join in. At morning the deer has been devoured, and the wolves are all safely back inside.

At last, in the middle of the night, Nine succumbs to Ten's insistence, and Seven knows that she must follow.

March 29

When the wolf team climb to their downwind observation point in the morning, they see: The Rose Creek pen is empty. There are wolf tracks down toward the road about half a mile, to an old elk carcass crumpled in the snow—winter kill, never touched by human hands but nonetheless suspicious enough that the wolves wouldn't touch it either. The deer that the team dropped last week, however, the day when Ten howled them down off his mountain—that has been quite thoroughly consumed, and by wolves. The footprints lead from the remains of the deer back up the narrow creek and over the ridge to where the snow blows everything blank, and there is no further trace. Telemetry from antennas rushed to nearby high points picks up nothing.

It is time for the team to take to the air.

While the Crystals still cringe inside their zone of security, the Soda Buttes have made an entirely different decision. Wolves are as different from one another as people. The Sodas are not only out, they're out in the middle of a wide treeless meadow, and in the golden light of late afternoon they are howling merrily, leaping and frisking, looking as wolfily comfortable as if they'd lived there all their lives.

March 30

Doug Smith's Piper Super Cub sweeps low up the Lamar River and its tributary Soda Butte Creek, and, no surprise, there are the Soda Butte wolves, not doing much of anything—touching noses, trotting here and there, one sitting on his haunches for a nice solo howl, another chasing a pair of coyotes away.

On the ground, Mike Phillips finds that the Sodas have been back inside the pen. He follows their tracks from there half a mile from there to where he can see they began to run, and then he comes on the body of an elk. Blood is everywhere. The rumen has been shoved aside—a reliable sign of a wolf kill. The canine tooth marks in the flesh are the span of those in wolves' mouths. They ate no more than ten percent of the meat before they moved on. This is the first wolf kill in Yellowstone in more than seventy years. Phillips fills out his kill form and takes a long happy look down the valley. It's working.

Nine, Ten, and Seven head north, and higher, into deeper snow, ruggeder rock. They have no idea where they are, but they begin to sense that it is not a good place for wolves.

Indeed it is not. Doug Smith picks up their radio signals in the remote headwaters of the Buffalo Fork—deep inside the Absaroka-Beartooth Wilderness, exactly in the worst direction. They are already at eight thousand feet, well above the winter range of any prey except a few scattered moose, and if they continue north—toward home?—the going will only get worse.

North, northwest, northeast, it is nothing but a world of rock and ice: the jagged Absaroka Mountains and the Beartooth Plateau, ten thousand feet above sea level, eleven here, twelve there, some of the most fearful landscape in North America even in summer, a land of year-round snowstorms, pitiless wind, sheer chasms, thousand-foot slides of unanchored scree, cracking glaciers in which grasshoppers twenty centuries old are still frozen, a land, in winter, of virtually nothing alive—a land, therefore, of nothing for a wolf to eat.

It is a world like nothing these Canadian wolves have ever known. Yet could they traverse it? They could. They're wearing dense fur coats. Their long legs can propel them through mile after mile of deep snow. Their big feet often keep them on top of snow that the less well-equipped—elk, for example, and deer—must crunch through. Evolution has fitted their metabolism to boom and bust: They can gorge themselves till they are round as bears, and nearly starve after that sometimes for weeks.

But it would be a bad idea. Where at last the alpine heights give way to forest, the mountains and canyons are steep and still clogged with snow and, at this time of year, still devoid of wolf prey. Assume for the moment that the wolves succeeded in struggling through that. They would then be almost fifty miles from the security of the national park. The canyons to the north and east open into river valleys, and the forests give way to savanna where the mountain winds blow the grasslands free of snow. There at last would be in elk winter range—hundreds of elk, drawn up into herds—but they would also be facing one very big problem. Much of that feast is on private ranch land, and the elk are often in the midst of herds of cattle, which bear their calves in late winter.

Nine and Ten have never seen a cow, or a calf. They have never seen a cattle ranch. It might not take them long, however, to figure out how easily caught and killed those spindly little morsels are. And under the terms of the wolf reintroduction, ranchers are fully empowered to shoot wolves preying on their livestock.

Even if they resisted that temptation and continued north, these wolves would not find a world much to their liking. They've seen cars, one or two from time to time, but never a town, never an Interstate highway. Home would probably be as unreachable as the moon. There is so much they do not know.

March 31

Smith flies again. Somewhat to his relief, Nine, Ten, and Seven remain in the same crazy place. It's too high and cold to find prey, but at least they're not heading north.

April 1

They have not moved.

April 2

They have not moved. This makes no sense.

April 3

And then at last, in the middle of the night, they turn south, downhill, back into the national park, then eastward and upstream along the Lamar River, and then away from the road up into its safe, elk-filled tributary valley, Cache Creek—a twenty-three-mile trip in the dark. No one bursts into tears, quite, but the sighs of relief, the hands clapped to cheeks, the groans of "Thank God" make clear how tense these days have been.

Seven has peeled off and is heading vaguely toward the Crystal Bench pen, where young male Two has remained behind, whiling away day after day doing absolutely nothing. There has been a certain amount of barely spoken enthusiasm for a potential match between these two young wolves, but Two has now chosen the perfectly wrong moment to make his first excursion into the outside world. As Seven approaches—with Two's scent rich in her nostrils—he is nowhere to be found.

That night in the Lamar, all three packs are howling. Can it be said yet that they are proclaiming themselves to be at home? Have they already begun to set up three separate territories?

April 4

Nine and Ten have traveled a short distance up the Lamar, nothing crazy, nothing dangerous. Nine's daughter Seven is back near the Rose Creek Pen.

Five of the six Crystals are also traveling together, quite near Nine and Ten, and also missing one youngster. Their young male Two is off on his own, way downstream on the Yellowstone River.

The Sodas continue to maintain strict family unity, four miles north of the Soda Butte Pen.

This is all to the good.

April 5, 6, 7

Three days of storm ensue, and the tracking plane is grounded. When at last, fighting the buffeting upsurges and cross-slaps still roiling the air, Doug Smith attempts a flight, he finds the Soda Butte and Crystal Bench packs minding their own business in same general vicinities where they were last seen, but Nine and Ten have moved back north into the high, bad winterlands north of the park boundary where they had so long and pointlessly bivouacked. Seven is in upper Rose Creek, perhaps on their trail. The weather becomes unbearable, and Smith returns, dipping and lurching, wings flapping unhappily, to the gravel strip at Gardiner.

Biologist Rolf Peterson examines the remains of a coyote killed by wolves.

April 8, 9, 10

Worse weather follows, and again no flying is possible.

What everyone has dreaded—but does not yet know—is true. Nine and Ten are in fact headed north. Plunging through snowdrifts, clawing their way across open granite shelves at ten thousand feet and higher, but most importantly trying to stay downwind along the sheer walls of the Beartooth's countless rock blades and dark crevices, they have no slightest sense of where they are, but something is pulling them northward.

April 11

Young Seven seems to have been drawn back south toward the pen. Doug Smith picks up her signal in the upper reaches of Rose Creek. But to find Nine and Ten he must fly well to the north, to Frenchy's Meadow, which in summer is a popular backcountry fishing destination and grizzly bear haunt but now is ice-locked nothingness, a way station at best.

April 12

Unflyable.

April 13

Nine and Ten are still at Frenchy's. A cow moose and her calf are bedded nearby, but the wolves seem not to have disturbed them. This would indicated that the mother moose is in good condition. Wolves know better than to attack an animal that big if she can fight back.

April 14

Bad weather again. Typical of Yellowstone at this time of year.

April 15

No flight.

April 16

The weather has improved, but it's Easter Sunday and the pilot refuses to fly. The biologists are furious.

April 17

The morning weather is bad, but begins to break up. Doug Smith attempts a flight in the afternoon but has to turn back when heavy clouds close in.

April 18

The weather clears. Smith flies hour on hour, sweeping his antenna back and forth and back and forth across the immensity of northern Yellowstone and the Absaroka-Beartooth Wilderness—the Absarokas black and jagged volcanics, the Beartooths silver granite, some of the worst winter weather on earth. The few creatures capable of withstanding the wind and ice here are sparse, rarely seen, armored in dense fur: wolverine, fisher, snowshoe hare, an endemic fox so rare that no one is quite sure if it still exists in the Yellowstone ecosystem.

There is no signal from the radio collars of Nine or Ten. None.

April 19

Seven shows up, astonishingly, in the heart of Yellowstone Park, at Tower Junction, and she has killed an elk, apparently all by herself—nearly unbelievable, yet undeniable. No sign of her mother, however, or stepdad. It has been eight days since they were last located.

The Crystal pack suddenly appears in an equally unbelievable place—on Beartooth Butte, far outside the park, far from anywhere with a decent hope of winter prey. The only thing about Beartooth Butte that could possibly make sense is that it lies to the north.

April 20

All morning the sky is low and gray. Wind slaps the thin hangar walls. Flying is impossible. Smith paces up and down. At last the weather breaks a little, and he takes hastily to the air.

He finds the Sodas still on their best behavior, no more than a few miles north of their pen. He must fly far to the north before he finds the Crystal Creek wolves. They have traveled twenty miles from Beartooth Butte since yesterday, in the worst possible direction. They have dropped down off the north edge of the Beartooth Plateau and are still headed north, along a ridge above the deep narrow canyon of Rock Creek. If this were a hundred years ago, they might have found extensive elk winter range where the canyon mouth opens to the prairies. Now, unfortunately, they will find the town of Red Lodge, Montana.

Smith flies from Hayden Valley, in the center of Yellowstone Park, to the east side of the Absarokas and north up Slough Creek, up the Buffalo Fork, up Hellroaring, down the east, west, and main forks of the Boulder River, up the Stillwater River, down Rock Creek off the Beartooths, across the elk-thronged Northern Range, up the Paradise Valley to Livingston and still farther along the Yellowstone River, as far east and north as Big Timber, Montana. Still Nine and Ten cannot be found.

Dave Mech has been thinking about the effects of stress on wolf reproduction. "I once had a group of four that I held in a pen at the height of the mating season. There was lots of copulation, but no pups." He pauses, ever judicious. "I don't want to generalize too much. There's so much variation among wolves, among packs, among populations."

What neither Mech nor anyone else wants to bring up is that the best candidates for parenthood are Nine and Ten. The other packs' restless movements are not suggestive of denning. Only Nine and Ten have exhibited the full gamut of mating behavior, and the way they seemed to cling to one space high in the snowbound mountains, though it may not have seemed wise, did suggest that Nine was slowing down. And now their apparent disappearance—couldn't that also mean that they are seeking shelter in some deep declivity, some cave, some fastness so remote that no radio collar's signal escapes it?

Or something worse.

Tomorrow the wolf team will bring out two airplanes.

April 21

A call comes in from Red Lodge. An agent of the Montana Department of Fish, Wildlife and Parks has seen what he believes to be wolf tracks in the snow, just outside of town.

Cold dread grips the biologists' hearts. This is too far. Why should any of these wolves have abandoned the prey-rich and unpeopled elk winter ranges, unless they think they are headed back to Canada?

On the other hand, Red Lodge is better than Hinton. And only living wolves leave tracks.

The two airplanes lie in readiness at Gardiner, prepared to sweep back and forth across the entire northern Yellowstone region, and beyond if need be. Till now the biologists have been flying up and down the major drainages, basing their routes on what they believe they know of likely wolf travel patterns, which typically follow waterways or ridgetops. Now they will fly higher, on a comprehensive grid that will leave no tiniest creek or slope unsearched. But the weather is gusty, low, unflyable.

April 22

The weather is still rotten, but Doug Smith cannot keep himself on the ground. Late in the day, wrenched and rocked in the angry wind, he flies back and forth across the snowy mountains, dark canyons, wide prairies. What he finds does no one's soul good.

Nine's daughter Seven has also left Yellowstone Park. She has headed due north up Hellroaring Creek into the Absaroka-Beartooth Wilderness, and she is still moving north.

And now the Sodas—the good, predictable, home-loving Sodas—have left the park as well, and to the north. They are already twenty miles north of the park boundary and are still going. They have passed over the crucial drainage divide separating parkward-flowing waters from north-flowing streams, and are moving down the drainage of the Stillwater River, which shoots through a steep wilderness canyon, largely devoid of game, until it begins to slow and meander through open grassland—private land, ranches. North of that lie many miles of easily passable prairie. There is not a significant topographic barrier between the Soda Butte pack and the land of their birth. There are, however, plenty of people with guns.

The weather over Red Lodge keeps it unapproachable, so Smith cannot locate the Crystals, and Nine and Ten are still unfound.

Of the fourteen wolves brought to Yellowstone in January, only one, Number Two, the timid Crystal Creek pup, remains inside the national park.

Another storm rips through Yellowstone, wind whipping, snow spitting, tailed by an icy stillness. Low, shapeless clouds settle into the Lamar, and all the valley turns pale. It is very cold, nearing zero by dusk, the sky breaking pink here and there, no fretful coyotes howling now, a faint dust of fresh snow. Elk emerge from the forest edge first in dozens, soon in scores, till hundreds spread themselves across the valley floor, and long shadows of the highlands swallow the last light.

April 23

Between the hardscrabble towns of Washoe and Bearcreek, Montana, a rutted two-track ranch road climbs south up Scotch Coulee toward an old stagecoach line known as the Meeteetsee Trail, which rounds the muddy northern flanks of Mount Maurice and then descends to cross windswept deserts to the east and south. Mount Maurice is a massive mountain, both broad and tall, and it dominates the skyline south of the town of Red Lodge. Across the Bearcreek highway to the north lie the ruins of the Smith coal mine, the site of Montana's deadliest industrial disaster, an underground fire that killed seventy-four men in 1943.

Scattered here and there from Washoe to Bearcreek and beyond, abandoned mining shacks are rotting into the earth. Only a few decrepit houses remain occupied.

The sparse grass is beginning to green. The snow that has brushed the Rock Creek canyon and Red Lodge over the ridge to the west did not come this far into the weather shadow of the Beartooth Plateau. Snow rarely does. Neither does rain. Neither do people. Under the overcast a few steers graze through the rabbitbrush and greasewood.

Red Lodge averages twenty-one inches of precipitation a year. Here on Bear Creek, only a few miles to the east, the average is eight. This is a land of dry washes and yellow clay buttes, of silences, wind, space, anonymity.

Chad McKittrick, an intermittently employed jack-of-few-trades from Red Lodge, turns out of the highway onto the Scotch Coulee track in a blue 1988 Ford four-wheel-drive pickup. At this wettest moment of the year, the ruts are aswim in brown water. The truck grinds slowly uphill past rusting mining equipment, broken bottles, a ruined railroad spur. A narrow feeder creek comes gurgling through a culvert beside which generations past caring have dumped their junk. A little unpainted cabin clings to the brushy hillside, home to a man named Dusty Steinmasel, a friend of Chad McKittrick's.

Past the cabin, the grade grows steeper, and the road deteriorates.

The soil is deep and fine-grained, the mud adhesive. Slipping, yawing, the truck claws up toward the high woodside meadows on the northeast face of Mount Maurice where black bears graze in the spring. This is private land, and McKittrick does not have permission to hunt here, a fact that does not deter him. He has bear on his mind, a spring bear-hunting license in his pocket, and a scope-mounted Ruger M-77 seven-millimeter magnum rifle on the seat beside him.

Fishtailing, slinging mud clods from its spinning wheels, the truck founders, dead stuck. Chad McKittrick gets out and contemplates the brown-spattered fenders, the wheels sunk axle-deep. There is nothing else to do, in the gathering dusk, but shoulder his rifle, grab some beer, and hike the two miles down to Dusty Steinmasel's cabin.

It is a Sunday evening, and Steinmasel is at home. "Pickup's high-centered up on the mountain," says McKittrick, twisting two cans out of the six-pack he has brought.

"How come I'm not surprised?" Steinmasel has known him since high school in Red Lodge.

They try to free McKittrick's truck in the dark, but Steinmasel's Jeep Cherokee is no match for the April muck. After they finish off the beer he drives McKittrick home, and they agree to try again in the morning with McKittrick's other rig and some proper equipment.

April 24, 1995

Early morning, first light bright and clear. Mike Phillips and his pilot sweep low over the Beartooths in the welcome windlessness, and praise be, the Soda Butte pack seem to have continued down the Stillwater only as far as the Stillwater mining complex. One good look at that, apparently—with its buildings, adits, heaps of platinum and palladium ore, settling ponds, houses, and round-the-clock light and noise—and the good old park must have come in for reconsideration, for they are rapidly backtracking. And as if by magic the Crystals are doing the same: Having had a look at Red Lodge and environs, they too seem to be expressing a preference for places high, cold, and lonely. Almost step for step they are following themselves in reverse up and over the ice-blasted heights of the Beartooth Plateau, across the Beartooth Highway and the upper Clark's Fork of the Yellowstone, around Hurricane Mesa, and finally to the ridge above Crandall Creek—precisely where they camped last week. If they continue this way, they will soon be back in the Lamar. Seven, too, has turned around, and come back down Hellroaring Creek. She is less than a mile above the park boundary.

The movements north, the simultaneous returns—the coordination is an utter mystery.

The ceaseless buzzing of the little yellow airplane circling and circling above him annoys Number Ten. He himself is walking in restless circles, peering down toward the green lands below, where, surely, there will be deer at last, perhaps even elk. But Nine is so tired she can hardly lift herself to her feet. Her belly is bulging with babies aching to be born. Ten knows that Nine needs to dig a den, or at least to find shelter.

Inside the yellow airplane, Mike Phillips is on the radio, "I've got them! I can see them! And they're fine. Mount Maurice, north slope. Only ten miles from Red Lodge, but I don't think they're moving north, I think they've stopped. Ten keeps walking around and around in circles, and Nine's not moving at all. I think she may be going to den right here."

Later, back in the office, Phillips reflects on Nine and Ten's location. "I'm supposed to be restoring wolves to the Greater Yellowstone Ecosystem," he says grimly. "I think you could question whether where Nine and Ten are is even inside the ecosystem. And it's nothing but downhill and wide open to the north and the east. Nothing but people and ranches and cattle and trouble."

Chad McKittrick and Dusty Steinmasel, in McKittrick's num-
ber-two truck, a green 1978 Ford, return at seven-thirty in the morning to the mired pickup on Mount Maurice. They come armed with
lumber, chains, shovels, axes, pry bars, a handyman jack, and McKittrick's customary just-in-case firepower, including a forty-four-caliber
magnum revolver, a twenty-two rifle, and the Ruger seven-millimeter
rifle. They pile one-by-sixes and two-by-sixes behind the tires and try
to wedge them beneath the tires. With wheels spinning and motor
roaring, McKittrick rocks the blue truck back and forth as Steinmasel
pulls with the green one. Steinmasel looks up to see a small, yellow
single-engine airplane circling above them.

They don't say much as they grow angrier. McKittrick thinks
Steinmasel isn't pulling his weight. Steinmasel considers McKittrick
a helpless, useless wimp.

After an hour and a half of struggle, the stuck blue truck slithers
free, and the mud-stained men, tempers cooling, sit quietly inside it
for an early-morning beer.

"Well, we got her."

"Yeah, we did." Steinmasel holds a long pause. "I don't know
what the hell you was doing up here in the first place, Chad."

"Hunting, man. Bear hunting."

"It's posted land."

"Yeah, well."

"Yeah, well."

McKittrick is forty-one years old, pale, burly, high-cheekboned,
short-necked, mustachioed, bald beneath his battered felt cowboy
hat. He wears thick glasses over his narrow blue eyes. Steinmasel,
forty-three, is as dark as McKittrick is pale, big, broad-shouldered,
clean-shaven, with long, luxuriant brown hair pulled into a ponytail;
he looks rather like an Indian but is not. McKittrick walks lightly,
delicately. Steinmasel tends to lumber. They have both been around
Red Lodge on and off since high school, seeing each other from time
to time at the Snow Creek Saloon or another of the bars along Broadway—casual friends, no more, with not much in common but their

station near the bottom of the continually upward-stretching socioeconomic scale of Montana.

Steinmasel works as a laborer for a concrete company. Divorced, but a good father to his two kids, he works hard and keeps out of trouble. He is a bow hunter, a sportsman. McKittrick drifts in and out of trouble, in and out of jobs—freelance carpenter, oilfield roughneck, firewood cutter, collector of shed antlers. He is also a collector of firearms; some in Red Lodge call him a gun nut. He is a lifelong bachelor, a regular at the Snow Creek Saloon, a friendly fellow who drinks a lot. He is a renegade from a strict Mormon family; two of his brothers were missionaries.

McKittrick starts the truck.

"Chad, look!" whispers Steinmasel hotly, pointing up the hill at something moving.

The door flies open, and McKittrick runs to the green truck and pulls out the Ruger. He settles the rifle butt against his shoulder and sights through the scope, which is set at a magnification of five.

"That's a wolf, Dusty," he says. "I'm going to shoot it."

"Are you sure?" says Steinmasel. "It might be a dog."

"No," says McKittrick, "it's a wolf."

"Chad, no," pleads Steinmasel. "What if it's somebody's dog?"

"Yeah, right," says McKittrick. He takes aim.

About a hundred and forty yards away, Wolf Number Ten is walking slowly along the ridgeline, silhouetted clearly against the sky.

Steinmasel rummages for his binoculars. Just as he gets them into focus, he hears the shot.

Nine sees Ten spin around, bite at the wound high on his back, fall, kick his legs twice, and then lie still. She runs to him. He is still breathing. She sees the men far down the hill. She knows what a rifle is. She knows that she must run and hide, and she does.

"*Why?*" Steinmasel cries out, the single word torn from deep in his chest.

Mount Maurice, near Red Lodge, Montana.

Chad McKittrick's truck got stuck in the mud here. He was standing beside it when he shot Number Ten on April 24, 1995. U.S. Fish and Wildlife Service agent Tim Eicher took these photographs three days later, just after recovering Number Ten's radio collar.

The man in the picture is standing precisely where Number Ten was when Chad McKittrick shot him.

The seven-millimeter magnum bullet has struck Number Ten in the upper chest cavity and ripped out through the other side, leaving massive lung hemorrhage and a shredded liver in its wake.

McKittrick lays down the rifle and takes up his forty-four magnum pistol for the coup de grâce, but by the time McKittrick and Steinmasel reach him, Ten is dead.

There is no question now. This is not a dog. Ten is wearing a radio collar imprinted with the words NATIONAL PARK SERVICE and HINTON, ALBERTA. In each of the wolf's ears is a red plastic tag marked FWS in white letters on one side and 10 on the other.

"This is a big fucking deal, Chad," says Steinmasel, who is scared, disgusted, and on the verge of throwing up. "We need to go to town and find somebody from Fish and Game and report this."

"No," replies McKittrick, only now beginning to realize the seriousness of his impulsive shot, "we can't report this. I'll go to jail. I can't do time."

"If we're not going to report it," Steinmasel tells his friend, "you're on your own." He feels his heart pounding. "I don't have nothing to do with this. If we report it, I'm behind you a hundred percent. I'm a witness. It's an accident."

"No," McKittrick insists. "I could go to jail."

Steinmasel and McKittrick agree on one thing—more beer. They rattle down to the tiny crossroads town of Belfry, Montana, for a twelve-pack.

On the way to Belfry, it occurs to them that the wolf's radio collar is undoubtedly still transmitting. Steinmasel reminds McKittrick about the little yellow plane that was circling above them this morning. They better go back through the backcountry, and quick. They jounce along the rutted old Meeteetsee Trail up to just below the ridge where Ten lies dead.

Steinmasel hikes up to get the carcass, thinking he'll carry it downhill. But Ten is way too heavy to lift—even now, after his arduous journey over the mountains, at least a hundred and ten pounds—so Steinmasel drags him. "Here's your wolf," he says to McKittrick. "What are you going to do with him?"

"I want him," says McKittrick. "Let's take him down to your garage and skin him."

"No fucking way, Chad," replies Steinmasel.

"Well, we can't just leave him lay here."

Steinmasel takes a wrench and unbolts and removes the radio collar. McKittrick clips off the red plastic ear tags. Together they lift Ten's body into the bed of the pickup.

McKittrick drives downhill till he finds a dense grove of cottonwood and willow that will conceal them. There they string the corpse up with orange baling twine. Sawing through the dense neck fur, the leathery skin, the amazingly strong muscle and dense bone, McKittrick cuts off Ten's head. He wants the skull.

Then he goes to work skinning the body. McKittrick is not much of a skinner, and Steinmasel grows impatient. He keeps thinking about that plane. If it's one of those tracking planes, whoever was in it could follow the radio signal and see them from the air right now. Steinmasel takes over to finish the skinning. They pick up Ten's blood-slick carcass by its big, densely furred feet and heave it into the brush at the foot of a red clay bank.

"At least let me hose down the cape at your house?" asks McKittrick.

Outside Steinmasel's cabin McKittrick takes the garden hose and sprays the blood from the raw pink underside of Ten's skin and from his own arms and hands.

"I'll take care of the collar," says Steinmasel. "Smash it or something."

McKittrick stuffs Number Ten's head and hide into a plastic garbage bag, slings it into the bed of his blue truck, and drives home. Steinmasel follows in McKittrick's green truck.

Behind McKittrick's house stands a cabin that he has been building a bit at a time, whenever there comes a little money and he has the energy. In the cold of the half-built cabin, where it will not spoil, Steinmasel helps McKittrick drape the wolf skin over a stepladder.

"We're right here," says Steinmasel. "Let's report it."

Chad McKittrick took the head and hide of Wolf Number Ten. This was all that was left.

"No," replies McKittrick, "I can't do it."

"Will you at least leave me out of it? Like, a gentleman's agreement?"

"Okay. Sure." They shake hands on it.

McKittrick drives Steinmasel back to the cabin in Scotch Coulee.

Steinmasel tries yet again. "Chad, we can go up the canyon and take care of this right now"—meaning bring the carcass down and call the authorities.

"I'm going bear hunting," is McKittrick's only reply.

Steinmasel knows that McKittrick is bullshitting again.

As night falls, Dusty Steinmasel sits in his house staring at the radio collar. He does not know that when a Telonics collar has not moved for more than five and a half hours, its usual rate of forty beeps per minute leaps to a rapidfire hundred-plus. Even a sleeping animal moves around a little from time to time, so when the faster signal

Dusty Steinmasel removed Ten's radio collar and threw it into a creek. He did not know that it was still broadcasting—in mortality mode.

comes in, you know that either the collar has somehow come off or the wearer is dead. The signal is known as mortality mode.

Steinmasel assumes that the radio collar is still transmitting, and he knows that unless he destroys it it is going to continue. He gets out his world atlas and looks up Hinton, Alberta.

He hears a vehicle. He sees the lights. His chest clenches like a heart attack. It is only his neighbor, Dave, driving down out of Scotch Coulee.

He cannot live with this fear. He is in too deep already. He cannot bring himself to smash the radio collar. He wipes it down to get the fingerprints off. In the dark he walks down the rutted road toward the highway, to the culvert where the runoff-swollen creek rushes through. He drops the collar in. He does not know if the signal can be heard from under water, but he hopes it can. He wants Chad McKittrick to be caught. He wants to be caught himself.

By the light of the sliver of waning moon, Number Nine picks her way downslope, avoiding the patches of snow in which her steps would leave clear prints. Her nose leads her to a red clay bank, thick brush, and what remains of her mate: the meat of his body, his four big feet. His head is gone.

She begins to dig into the bank, faster and faster. She digs until she cannot go on. She lies beside the body of Number Ten and sleeps.

The urgency of imminent birth sets her to digging again at first light. But a pickup truck approaches, growling and making metal noises, and she must shrink away upslope into a stand of lodgepole pine. When the truck leaves, she returns to her den. A storm is blowing in, hard-edged and cold, keeping flies away from Ten's body. Another truck comes. She lies very still, waiting, waiting. A man descends and comes near, peering into the brush. She holds her breath. He goes away.

This will not do. She cannot stay here. Cramped with pain, she struggles back toward the heights and dense timber. She clears a rough bowl beneath the low boughs of a spruce tree, and she has barely lain down when the pups begin to come.

April 25

Snow clouds blow in from the west. White ice-edged gusts whip against quivering aluminum wings at the Gardiner airstrip. Smith and Phillips sit by the phone, waiting for the weather to clear. It does not clear.

April 26

The next morning is rough but flyable. Smith sweeps across the north face of Mount Maurice to the coordinates where Phillips last saw Nine and Ten, two days ago. He picks up Nine's signal easily, although he cannot see her. Ten's signal, however, is faint, and vague, it seems to be coming from nowhere specific, which is strange. For a moment then he hears it clearly. The too-fast beeping. Mortality mode.

This can't be right. The wolf must have slipped his collar. Then somebody found it and took it inside a building, which would explain why the signal is so vague. Lot of buildings along Rock Creek. Smith flies up and down the creek, but the signal fades away. It comes back again, weakly, as he returns to the road below Mount Maurice, the ruined mine, the beat-up houses. He circles and circles, disbelieving, saying to himself, *No*, over and over, *no, no, no*, until he is running out of gas. He picks Ten's signal up once more, and this time it's clear. Mortality mode.

At park headquarters all hell breaks loose. Washington has to be called. The Carbon County sheriff. Fish, Wildlife and Parks. Fish and Wildlife Service, both the biologists and now the law enforcement arm. The highway patrol, to block the roads.

The Park Service, true to form, orders its public information officers to release no information to the public.

The weather is closing in, and flying again now is impossible. Mike Phillips and Doug Smith, in a Park Service SUV, race toward the scene at harrowing speed. The road is narrow, icy in unexpected spots, treacherous. Smith is saying, "This could be a false alarm, transmitter malfunction, maybe the collar's just lying on the ground." Phillips, eyes fixed on the road, says nothing, driving as hard as he can. It takes them almost three hours to reach Red Lodge.

At the Carbon County courthouse they meet Fish and Wildlife Service biologist Joe Fontaine, sheriff Al McGill, a couple of Montana game wardens, and Tim Eicher, a Fish and Wildlife Service law enforcement agent, to form a search team.

Everybody looks to Eicher, who has long experience of potentially dangerous poachers. "We don't even know if we have a crime here," he begins. "If we do, it could be one person or half a dozen. First thing we got to do is find that collar." Eicher looks at his watch.

There are only a few hours of daylight left.

"Supposed to snow tonight," a deputy says. "That won't help."

Doug Smith spreads out a topographic map. "My coordinates are not very good," he says gloomily. "I never did get much of a signal."

"We're just going to have to spread out," says Eicher, "and give it a try."

Everyone fears, though no one says, that if they do not find Ten this afternoon they will never find him. All it takes is a good hammer, to smash the collar, and a shovel, to bury the body.

The sheriff, several deputies, the wardens, and Eicher trudge along the transect that Eicher has roughed out for them, trying to cover the area as thoroughly as they can, poking into brush and garbage, sweeping their flashlights back and forth as daylight fails. Joe Fontaine tries his antenna from various high points but gets nothing. Finally they agree to bag it for the night. The locals go home. Fontaine and Eicher find motel rooms and some restless sleep.

Smith and Phillips stay out listening on a high ridge until eleven, hoping perhaps to pick up Nine's signal. Smith drives back to Gardiner so he can fly in the morning.

April 27

At first light Smith takes to the air. Old, grainy snow streaks the greening foothills of Maurice, but there is only a thin veil of new-fallen. The evidence, therefore, if any is to be found, remains unburied. Smith tunes in to Nine's frequency, and there she is! He can actually see her—vivid against the snow, in a small clearing in the woods on the north slope of the mountain, no more than five miles from Red Lodge, exactly where she was three days ago with Ten.

Damn, says Smith to himself, what a terrible place to den.

Now the Super Cub wheels northeastward, and Smith switches his receiver to 216.190, Number Ten's frequency. The signal is somewhat muffled, but louder and clearer than yesterday. It is still in mortality mode. Again Smith cannot home in on the precise location—maybe the signal is ricocheting, maybe the collar is indoors or under something—but as he tunes in from different angles he grows certain that the radio signal is coming from somewhere in the valley of Bear Creek.

As soon as he lands at Gardiner, Smith hastily draws a map, showing as well as he can where he thinks the collar may be, and faxes it over to Red Lodge. Now Sheriff McGill, Tim Eicher, Joe Fontaine, and the state wardens can narrow the search for Ten on the ground. They drive over the snowy divide and down the Bearcreek highway into the desert. Joe Fontaine holds the antenna out the window of his pickup. As he nears a rutted old ranch road near the ruins of the Smith coal mine, the signal grows stronger. He motions for the team to pull off the highway.

The urgent beeping leads the search team south up a narrow, muddy track between sage-covered hills pocked with melting snow. Two hundred yards in, they come to a culvert beneath the road. The signal is now so intense that it is distorting in Fontaine's receiver and he must remove the aerial. Garbage and old mining debris are scattered up the hillsides and downstream. The spring runoff water is high, sluicing through the culvert fast and hard.

The signal is coming from somewhere in the culvert. "Let me do this," says Tim Eicher. He pulls on his rubber hip boots and goes in, hunched double against the rushing, painfully cold stream, feeling with his hands in the black water. As he comes back into the light at the upstream end of the culvert, Eicher's hands close on the radio collar.

Telonics radio collars are made to take a beating. The transmitter is encased in a waterproof fiberglass shell. The neck band is made of heavy double-layered leather, three inches wide and almost half an inch thick. Its ends overlap between two stainless steel plates secured with stainless steel nuts and bolts. "Well, gentlemen," says Eicher, holding out the collar for the gathered team to examine, "here's our evidence. This collar has been unbolted."

Now it is certain. Wolf Number Ten is dead.

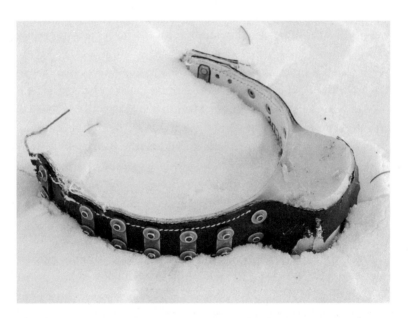

When a radio collar has been unbolted or sliced open, you know that there has been dirty work.

April 28

Doug Smith sits at his desk with his fingers pressed into his fore-head. "I had a personal attachment to that wolf," he says. "He was our star. And now Nine—she's in a very bad situation." He goes on to explain that in a pack, the whole family would be feeding her—masticating meat to a dense, high-protein pulp and then regurgitating right into her mouth. Ten alone could have been doing it, and much of that nutrition would have been going toward the production of milk. In time, the pups would have begun to share in the predigested prey, and then Nine would have been able to go out and hunt, with Ten home babysitting.

But if Nine were to leave her pups now and go off to hunt, they could be smelled out by a predator even in a deeply dug den. Coyotes are abundant here. Bears are only recently out of hibernation, and hungry. Even if perfectly hidden from predators, the tiny, thin-pelted newborns could easily die of hypothermia in this raw, wet weather. "On the other hand," says Smith, "if she doesn't hunt, her milk will dry up and the pups will starve."

April 29 –May 2

Interagency warfare of the bitterest and most ignoble sort breaks out over jurisdictional primacy. Joe Fontaine and the Fish and Wildlife Service argue for leaving Nine to den where she is. Mike Phillips, by way of reply, goes ballistic. "That is ridiculous! We're sup-posed to be establishing a wolf population in the Greater Yellowstone Ecosystem, not out on the plains of Montana!"

But it is one thing to decide to move Number Nine and another to do it. Consider what her experience of humankind is. In Canada she has seen her own pups snared, strung up, frozen to death, shot in the head—by people. She saw her living pup, Seven, trapped, drugged, taken away, then mysteriously released reeking of people. She herself then was trapped, drugged, prodded, invaded, locked in a steel box, imprisoned in roaring machines by people. When at last she could breathe air again, it was foreign air, and she found she was imprisoned again, behind chain-link fence, unable to run, unable to hunt, fed nothing but stinking dead meat—by people. A mate was chosen for her by people, she had no choice, and then he was killed by people.

How likely is it, now, that she will allow herself to be trapped by people?

May 3

Joe Fontaine climbs through the mottled, crumbling, knee-deep snow down the north face of Mount Maurice with a Telonics receiver and a hand-held antenna. When he picks up Number Nine's signal, he does not move straight toward her, but rather veers to the side, to get the signal from another bearing. Thus, by triangulation, he can locate her precisely without coming too close and disturbing her. He moves into the forest quiet as a cat.

The *tock-tock-tock* in Fontaine's headphones grows louder. He is homing in on her. She is close. Downhill, the snow has drifted deep, and the forest is thick where several small streams race out of the heights. Along these watercourses grow large Engelmann spruces and a dense riparian understory of alder, willow, bog birch, and hawthorn. Nothing as well hidden as a wolf bed will be visible once these deciduous plants come into leaf, which will be soon. Fontaine needs to find Nine soon.

It is about thirty-five degrees, and overcast. Fontaine can see the whole town of Red Lodge spread below him, not five miles away. He walks east, trying to circle wide around the wolf. He sees wolf tracks leading away, but they might not be fresh; he elects to stay with the greater immediacy of telemetry. He sees a day bed scooped into the snow, wolf-sized, near a tall old spruce tree.

He hears a faint mewing. He is three yards from the big spruce. Nine's signal is strong, but she seems to be moving away fast. He hears the mewing again, close, but still he cannot find it. He lifts a low, snow-hugging bough of the spruce tree. In the near-darkness back against the trunk he sees a squirming, whimpering mass of baby wolves—newborns, their eyes still closed. He counts seven, and thinks there may be eight.

Mike Phillips, at Yellowstone Park headquarters, is livid. "Nice job, Joe!" he cries to his invisible nemesis. "He's displaced her! She may abandon that litter. This is just great."

May 4

Joe Fontaine begins delivering roadkill to a spot near the big spruce where he found the pups, and it is soon apparent that Nine has returned. As the war of the agencies rages, at least she does not have to hunt.

The question of whether she is safe so close to where her mate was shot is keeping Mike Phillips's blood pressure high. "Mr. Bullet is still out there walking around! And where do you think those wolves are going to go as soon as they can travel? I'll lay money they're going to go north or east out onto those flats. What kind of future do you think they'll have out there, in the middle of people and houses and livestock? These wolves may be the only chance we ever get! We have absolutely no assurance that we're going to get more wolves next year. What's Nine supposed to do next February? Mate with a coyote? A dog?"

May 5—May 14.

While the bureaucrats and biologists argue, believing the situation of Nine and her brood to have more or less stabilized beneath the spruce tree, the local wolf-hating population of Red Lodge and environs are developing their I-told-you-so narrative: I told you the wolves weren't going to stay in the park. Didn't I tell you the feds was planning all along to plant 'em in the midst of us?

Fortunately the feds, worn out with arguing anyhow, take due note of that dangerously growing mood. They have also to consider the now established fact that the Soda Butte pack has produced a grand total of one pup and the Crystal Bench pack none. On Wolf Number Nine and her eight offspring, therefore, may depend the future of the wolf in Yellowstone.

And so the combatants come at last to agreement. Nine will be trapped and moved back to the park, along with her pups.

Meanwhile, however, Nine has been feeling crowded by all the human attention she has been getting. Not even slightly "stabilized," she has taken her pups in her mouth one by one and moved them half a mile upmountain through dense forest to another dark, hidden bowl of soft spruce needles. Even there, however, she does not feel safe, and after just two nights she carries the cubs to the edge of a steep slide of the broken rock known as talus. At the foot of a lone tree she scrapes out a rough depression in which she can curl up around the pups to nurse. In the event of disturbance she can tuck them into the interstices of the rock slide.

May 15

Nevertheless she must return to the established feeding site to eat. Doug Smith, Joe Fontaine, and Carter Niemeyer set five steel-jawed leghold traps into the ground along the route where Nine's tracks clearly show she always travels to the feeding site. They cover the traps with dirt and duff. This is a critical contest between Carter Niemeyer's expertise at the limit of its perfection—the most important trapping challenge of his life—and one wolf's determination to avoid it to the limit of her ability. Niemeyer has smeared each trap site with the feces of her dead mate, collected from the Rose Creek pen. He also has concocted his own personal magic potion for trapping wolves, a reeking secret formula which he paints on every surface possibly contaminated by human scent.

Each trap is connected by a string to a simple radio transmitter about the size of a flashlight. If the trap springs, the string will pull a magnet off the transmitter, and it will start emitting a rapidfire beep. These transmitters have been pirated from Telonics radio collars, so that what in its previous incarnation was mortality mode will now be good news.

Each radio transmits on a different frequency, and each will be checked every two hours around the clock. The night clerk at the Super 8 Motel in Red Lodge does the wolf team a welcome favor by volunteering to listen for the radio so that the biologists can catch a few hours of sleep.

For three nights straight Nine comes to feed hungrily on the feast of meat that Smith has brought from the park and that Niemeyer has placed so expertly near his traps. Does she suspect?

May 18

At four o'clock in the morning the cold steel jaws slam shut on Number Nine's leg. The pain is intense, but nothing compared to her terror. If you will attribute to a wolf a conception of the future, imagine Nine's despair. At first she screams in panic, then howls in agony, then slumps silent to the ground, certain that she is soon to die.

Mark Johnson hears the signal firing and shakes Doug Smith awake. "I don't want to handle her in the dark," whispers Johnson. "So let's take our time."

They wake the others, and all wait through the slow ticking minutes till they can fire up their vehicles and arrive at the trap at first light.

And by five-thirty a.m. Wolf Number Nine is fast asleep, with tranquilizer surging through her synapses and a blindfold to protect her eyes from bright light. A helicopter waits nearby. She gets a shot of penicillin and vitamins. Mark Johnson examines her and declares her to be in fine condition, though decidedly skinny. Despite the generous portions of elk and deer meat she has been served, her weight is down from the ninety-eight pounds she weighed at Hinton to eighty-five. Gently Johnson and Fontaine lift Number Nine into one of the original stainless steel shipping kennels and onto a bed of clean straw.

The trackers, including the excited clerk from the motel, now go in search of the pups. They follow Nine's trail to her recently established den site, which is little more, again, than a dug-out bowl in the snow beneath a tree, and oh, shit. The pups are not there.

Mike Phillips, once more, has had it up to here with Joe Fontaine. "You see?" Phillips seethes. "He's displaced her again."

For two hours, three, stretching into four, Fontaine leads the team on an anxious search for the big spruce under which he first found the pups, to which he hopes she may have returned them.

Doug Smith, on the other hand, is certain that the litter will not be there: "I've got several radio-locations of Nine in the same place, and it's nowhere near Fontaine's spruce tree."

Fontaine persists nonetheless. "This is my operation, isn't it?"

And it is, so the others go along. Finally they find the nest beneath the spruce tree. No pups. No sign of recent occupancy.

"You see?" says Phillips, taking no pleasure in being right.

At eleven-thirty in the morning, after six hours of slogging through melting snow and thick, adhesive mud, Fontaine woofs his soft maternal wolf-grunt for the thousandth time, and this time he hears, faintly, a whimpering.

"I've got it!" he whispers over his shoulder. The other members of the team hurry forward.

Fontaine has found the den, though it is hardly worthy of the term. This den is even more makeshift than the previous one—no more than a scooped-out depression beneath a ragged tree in a talus slide, obviously new, and made in haste. Surrounded by that jumble of broken rock, however, it is nonetheless intelligently placed, well protected.

The motherless pups flee clumsily but quickly at the sight of the dreadful invaders, wriggling into dark, deep spaces between the rocks. The terrified pups are not easy to get hold of. Sometimes the men must reach into some crack all the way up to their armpits. In time they have seven little wolves, but the eighth, if there is one, remains hidden and now silent in some crevice, nobody knows where. At last a probing stick touches something soft, yielding, breathing, definitely alive—could be a pika, a hibernating marmot, could be a baby wolf. The longest arm, Fontaine's, cannot quite reach. Doug Smith tries a pair of leatherman pliers. Stretching to the limit, with a man on each leg helping to ram him deeper into the crevice, Smith clamps hold of the soft fuzzy thing and drags Nine's eighth pup into the first day of her new life.

Mark Johnson examines the pups and draws a little blood from each. They all look fine—healthy, bright-eyed, squirming, squealing, making their dissatisfaction loudly apparent. Seven of them are black; one is brownish gray shading toward black. All weigh between four and five pounds. Four are male and four are female.

"We did it," says Johnson, watching the anger and fear drain from the eyes of his teammates.

The moment is too happy, and too grave, for further words.

The pups roam loose around the helicopter as Nine, now recovered from her drugging, sniffs at them from inside her metal box. The wolves and their unrecognized benefactors skim the Beartooth Plateau, the white, black, and blue winter wasteland of ice and rock spangled with frozen lakes. The dense forest of upper Soda Butte Creek rolls by beneath, and then the wide bright fast-greening meadows of the Lamar Valley.

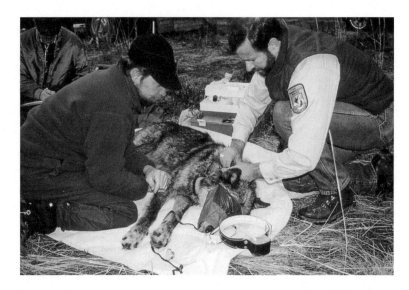

Mark Johnson and Joe Fontaine gave Number Nine a thorough medical exam immediately after her rescue. Sometimes an anesthetized wolf will open its dilated eyes, and bright light could damage them—hence the blindfold.

Joe Fontaine and Mark Johnson fit Number Nine with a new radio collar.

The pups were decidedly in danger on Mount Maurice, but veterinarian Mark Johnson pronounced all eight to be in fine shape.

One of Nine and Ten's just-found pups snuggles in for a helicopter ride to safety.

Mark Johnson with another of the pups, awaiting deliverance.

The helicopter comes to earth just outside the Rose Creek pen. The men stuff the pups one by one into the would-be den they have made inside the pen, a lean-to of logs and spruce boughs. They open the door of the kennel. Nine bounds out to kiss her family and breathe the well-remembered scent of what had better now be home.

III

April 27, 1995

A mud-spattered Jeep Cherokee turns in off the Bearcreek highway and stops at the search party. A long-haired fellow climbs out, blinking uneasily. "What's going on?" he asks.

Tim Eicher studies the guy intently: shoes, trousers, belt, shirt, jacket, hands, rings, height, weight, chin, mouth, nose, eyes, hair, hat. Steinmasel's cap bears the legend BACA LAND AND CATTLE COMPANY. Eicher once served eight years as a game warden in New Mexico, and by God, come to think of it, he remembers seeing this nervous son of a gun somewhere around there.

"I remember you," says Eicher, smiling, stepping forward with his hand out.

He remembers Eicher too. "Dusty Steinmasel," he says, not meeting Eicher's eyes, and points up the road beyond. "I live just up there."

"Seen anything unusual lately?" asks Eicher. "Anybody coming through? Particularly Monday?" Eicher believes that Ten was killed on Monday, April twenty-fourth, because the next day was too stormy and snowy for your typical lazy-ass poacher to be out and about.

"Nothing unusual," Steinmasel says, "nobody through here for at least a week. Just me and my neighbor,"

"Name of your neighbor?"

"Dave Oxford?"

Tim Eicher teaches interrogation techniques to up-and-coming officers, so he knows what to look for. "First," he says, "you have to decide which of three types of person you are dealing with: visual, auditory, or feeling. Your visual type will look upward when you question him, and tend to say things like 'I see.' The auditory person will tend to look sideways when you question him, and say something like, 'I hear you.' The feeling type tends to keep his eyes downcast, and his remarks will refer to his feelings." Eicher will not reveal his technique for determining whether the person is telling the truth or not, except to say that it has to do with involuntary eye movements—so involuntary that nobody can control them even if he knows the trick.

Eicher knows instantly that Steinmasel is lying.

A little later, Steinmasel's neighbor, Dave Oxford, the only other person living in Scotch Coulee, drops by to see what all the hubbub is about.

"Sir," Eicher asks Oxford, "have you seen anybody around or anything unusual?"

"Not really," says Oxford. Oxford's face is open, his eyes unevasive. "Oh—well, I did see Chad McKittrick on Monday, when Chad and Dusty went up the hill to get Chad's truck unstuck."

Ah.

Eicher walks up the road past Steinmasel's cabin and on uphill for a couple of miles till he comes to a place where he can see that a vehicle had been stuck in the mud. What his gut and his training has already told him, evidence now confirms: Dave Oxford was telling the truth, and Dusty Steinmasel was not.

May 2

Despite his Ohio birth, his Michigan education, and his master's degree in wildlife biology, U.S. Fish and Wildlife Service special agent Tim Eicher is the very image of the Western lawman. From the tip-top of his big cowboy hat or, if indoors, his gleaming bald dome, to his steady blue-eyed stare and his luxuriant handlebar mustache and down to the sharp-tipped toes of his high-heeled boots, everything about Eicher proclaims that this is not a man to be messed with. His voice is low, and hard. His words are spare, and precise.

Eicher's stiff-necked cop taciturnity, while real enough, is underlain by a quieter sense of antic humor, but what some wolf shooter is by God going to get is, in Eicher's own words, "a man hunter. And I don't fail. It may take time, but I get who I'm after. Always."

The Fish and Wildlife Service offers a reward of one thousand dollars for information leading to the conviction of the killer of Wolf Number Ten. Defenders of Wildlife adds five thousand more. The National Audubon Society adds five thousand. An organization in California called Sea Shepherd, whose portfolio is marine mammals, has for some reason kicked in two thousand more.

The tips, the leads, the rumors, the absolutely certain accusations are piling up on Eicher's desk in Cody, Wyoming. "It's too much fucking money," he complains. "When I get the guy, he's going to want a jury trial, and in a district where the median income is twenty thousand dollars, that thirteen thousand is going to be a problem. Any jury here is going to know people will lie for thirteen thousand dollars."

And why isn't Eicher prowling the bars of Red Lodge incognito, meeting with secret informants, Sherlock-Holmesing the scene of the crime? Why is he sitting behind his desk?

"Something will come up. A hunter has to be patient."

There is pressure on Tim Eicher. His bosses want this crime solved *now*. His phone rings not only with the fantasies of reward hunters and the lies of grudge bearers but also with ceaseless official and unofficial "encouragement" from the chain of federal command all the way up to Washington. And how does all that heat affect him?

Eicher leans back in his chair with his hands behind his head. Beneath the big mustache his lips part at the corner with a single soft smack, as though around an invisible toothpick. "I don't give a shit about pressure.

"See, look," he continues. "Ten's radio collar was hidden in that culvert, right? The only person who would think to throw it in there

U.S. Fish and Wildlife Service agent Tim Eicher is so cool he can ride past a grizzly bear without looking. His horse is even cooler. His name is Rock.

would be a local. And I'm pretty sure I know who it is, and I'm pretty sure all I have to do is wait. There's going to be one phone call," he says.

Of all the scores of calls Special Agent Time Eicher will have received, he will recognize this one. Late some remorse-ridden evening, that thirteen thousand bucks is going to draw Dusty Steinmasel to the telephone.

May 10

But Eicher is mistaken. Steinmasel does not call. Eicher is also kicking his own butt for not driving the Bearcreek highway right away. "I'd have seen birds over the carcass—ravens probably. Could have found it a lot sooner. Stupid mistake. And then a couple times when I was interrogating Dusty, when I should have been staring a hole in him, I was taking notes. Another mistake." Eicher's humility is the measure of his confidence.

A crack interrogator from the Denver office by the name of Leo "Grasshopper" Suazo flies in to join Tim Eicher for a little visit with Dusty Steinmasel.

Eicher adopts his coldest, flattest official tone. "Dusty, were you up the Scotch Coulee road on the evening of April twenty-third?" he demands.

"Nope."

"Were you up the Scotch Coulee road on the morning of April twenty-fourth, helping Chad McKittrick get his blue Ford truck unstuck?"

"No, sir."

"You know who killed that wolf, Dusty."

"Well, all right, I was up there with Chad that morning," Steinmasel admits with an exhalation of relief, followed by a quick tightening. "But I don't know who killed the wolf. I sure didn't."

Tim Eicher and Grasshopper Suazo share a flicker of eye contact. With an imperceptible nod they agree to end the interview abruptly. The special agents bid good-bye to a very rattled Dusty Steinmasel.

Eicher is one hundred percent certain, this time, that Steinmasel is going to call.

May 13

Steinmasel leaves a message on Eicher's answering machine, knowing that today, a Saturday, Eicher will not be in the office. "I forgot to tell you about the black Chevy," he says. He wants to talk.

Eicher picks up his messages and senses immediately that there is no black Chevy. He gets in his unmarked but typically obvious government truck and drives north into Montana, to Belfry—where Chad McKittrick and Dusty Steinmasel bought a twelve-pack of beer the morning of the killing of Wolf Number Ten—then west up the desolate Bearcreek highway to meet Steinmasel.

The man hunter is calm. The hunted man is tied up in knots. Steinmasel tells the story truthfully, Eicher believes, and in meticulous detail—right up to the moment when he and McKittrick are standing over Number Ten's body. At that point, he goes vague.

"After Chad shot the wolf, see, I went straight home," says Steinmasel, stammering a little, "and then I was so upset I went out, uh, fishing. I never handled the body. Or that radio collar. I went back to look at the wolf again that afternoon and it was gone."

"You went back," says Eicher. "And what did you notice when you went back?"

"There was new tire tracks."

"What did you notice about the tire tracks, Dusty?"

"They were leading uphill toward the Meeteetsee Trail."

Eicher knows that Steinmasel is lying about the afternoon, but he remains pretty sure that the details of the killing in the morning are true. He has enough information now for a search warrant on Chad McKittrick.

May 14

Dusty Steinmasel drives through Red Lodge and out to Chad McKittrick's house to confess that he has ratted on him. McKittrick is quiet, forgiving, and drunk.

"I left myself out of it," says Steinmasel, "just like we said in our gentlemen's agreement, you remember? I didn't say anything about helping you bring that carcass down the hill. I didn't say anything about helping you skin it. I didn't say anything about helping you bring it over here to the cabin. This is like we agreed, right, Chad?"

Dusty Steinmasel does not know that his false story concealing those facts is a federal felony.

McKittrick nods gloomily. "I'm sorry I got you involved," he says. "I've been out here drunk for the last two weeks while you been running around paranoid." He pauses for a long moment. "I'm glad it's over."

May 15

Tim Eicher and his supervisor, Commodore Mann (that is actually his name), appear in federal court in Billings, Montana. They present to Judge Jack Shanstrom an Application and Affidavit for Search Warrant. Eicher has laid out his case in six terse pages. "Based on the foregoing," the application concludes,

> the affiant has probable cause to believe that evidence of the illegal take, possession, and transportation of wolf #R10 will be found at the property of Chad McKittrick, located in Palisade Basin Ranches subdivision, Tract 21, near Red Lodge, Carbon County, Montana; said property being fruits, instrumentalities, and evidence of a violation of the

Endangered Species Act and the Lacey Act, and con-
sisting of a wolf hide, wolf hair and blood, a wolf
skull and/or wolf parts, a 7 mm magnum rifle and
7 mm ammunition, a leather rifle scabbard, knife(s),
axe(s), small metal plate(s) and two bolts, 1x6 and
2x6 boards, and orange baling twine, said property
being fruits, instrumentalities, and evidence of violations of the Endangered Species Act, 16 USC
1538(a)(G), 50 CFR 17.84(i)(3) and (5) and the
Lacey Act, 16 USC 3372(a)(1).

Warrant in hand, Eicher, Mann, and two other Fish and Wildlife
Service special agents, Roy Brown and Ron Hanlon, make for Red
Lodge, sixty miles away. There they meet sheriff McGill, Montana
Department of Fish, Wildlife and Parks agent Kevin Nichols, and a
sheriff's deputy who will sit in the car down the road for backup in
case of trouble. In convoy, they head for McKittrick's.

Thanks to Steinmasel's visit the previous night, McKittrick is
expecting them. He greets the intimidating contingent of lawmen
and firepower with what seems almost like gratitude. He also looks
jumpy in the extreme, and Eicher knows that nobody whose home is
being minutely searched for criminal evidence is likely to feel especially peaceful, and he knows that McKittrick is not Carbon County's
most stable individual. While the others comb through the house,
Eicher takes McKittrick out for a little walk-and-talk. Eicher does not
take notes, and he is not carrying a tape recorder. He is, however,
wearing a loaded pistol. They go down and check out the trout ponds.
They hit a few golf balls. "I'm not denying I shot that animal, you
know," says McKittrick forlornly. "I feel bad about it. But I thought
it was just a wild dog. Might kill a calf up there on that ranch."

"They do that," Eicher agrees amiably, not mentioning that
McKittrick was trespassing on the ranch or that there were no cattle
anywhere near.

"They will do that. Dogs. They will. Do you think I'm going to
be famous?"

Eicher manages not to smile. "A lot of people don't like the wolf reintroduction, Chad, but it's still a federal crime to kill a wolf."

"I thought it was a dog, sir."

Eicher does not pursue the possibility of Chad McKittrick becoming famous for killing a dog.

"I wonder if NBC might want to make a TV movie about me," McKittrick muses.

"I wish it could have been just him and me," Eicher later recalls, "without all those troops, the sheriff, old Commodore and all. When you're alone, confession can be like a secret between you. He was coming close."

Inside McKittrick's house, meanwhile, the officers find McKittrick's Ruger M-77 rifle under the sofa, with elk ivory embedded in the stock and three live rounds of ammunition in the magazine. Eicher brings McKittrick in, and the suspect escorts his captors to the wolf's hide and severed head on a ladder in the half-built cabin out back.

Chad McKittrick is charged with killing Wolf Number Ten, possessing the remains, and transporting them.

Ten's head, hide, and body will be frozen and then shipped to the U.S. Fish and Wildlife Service forensics laboratory at Ashland, Oregon. In the lab, forensic mammalogist Bonnie Yates will introduce the wolf's head into a colony of flesh-eating beetles, where it will stay until the skull is clean, white, and free of stink. She will then measure the cranium, jaw, and teeth. Her morphometry will confirm that it is the skull of a gray wolf.

Molecular biologist Stephen Fain will subject Ten's flesh and hair to three sorts of DNA testing. A nucleotide sequence analysis of mitochondrial DNA isolated from the body recovered at Scotch Coulee will determine that it can have come only from a member of the species *Canis lupus*. A polymerase chain reaction will prove that the dead wolf was a male. A comparison restriction analysis will show that the hide and head and flesh all belonged to the same animal, and also that the dead male wolf's DNA matches precisely that of the plug of flesh punched out of Number Ten's ear at Hinton and kept frozen for precisely such a situation as this.

Veterinary pathologist Richard Stroud will remove the tiny Personal Identification Tag from Number Ten's skin. The PIT tag, scanned by a laser-driven reader, will confirm the wolf's identity. An X-ray will find bullet fragments inside Ten's thorax in a pattern typical of a high-powered rifle wound. Stroud will find that the shrapnel completely destroyed the wolf's liver and lungs. The greater part of the bullet continued on through the abdomen and out the other side. It has never been found.

May 30

Tim Eicher gets an anonymous call suggesting that Dusty Steinmasel may have more still to tell. Eicher goes to Steinmasel's house and asks him, "What the hell's going on, Dusty?"

Steinmasel has been writing—the whole story, including all of his own involvement. He doesn't want the reward, he says, and he's not looking for a deal. Just wants to clear his conscience.

"Sign it," says Eicher.

Steinmasel does so, and Eicher takes it away.

June 12

Coming too fast around a curve in the mountains near Cooke City, Montana, Chad McKittrick—free on bail—careens off the Beartooth Highway and rolls his truck. The highway patrol takes a while coming from Red Lodge over the Beartooth Pass, which at almost eleven thousand feet is still snow-packed and icy even in mid-June. By the time they arrive, McKittrick has crawled out of the wreckage and gotten a lift to Cooke. He is now in one of the bars, drunk. Because it cannot be determined whether he got drunk in the bar or was already drunk when he had the accident, McKittrick will not be charged with driving under the influence.

He is wearing a big knife, two pistols, and a T-shirt emblazoned with the words NORTHERN ROCKIES WOLF REDUCTION PROJECT— a witty gift from one of his drinking buddies at the Blue Ribbon Bar in Red Lodge. The cab of his pickup is full of beer bottles. The officers confiscate a total of nine guns.

After calling in his license number, the highway patrolmen learn that the man is facing federal charges for killing a wolf. They never report the accident, the T-shirt, the nine firearms, or any of McKittrick's other numerous and blatantly apparent violations of the law.

July 4

Chad McKittrick rides his horse in the Independence Day parade down Broadway in Red Lodge wearing his NORTHERN ROCKIES WOLF REDUCTION PROJECT T-shirt and carrying a loaded pistol. After the parade, he rides the horse into a bar.

Later in the summer, McKittrick attends Quarter Beer Night— twenty-five cents per beer, that is—at the Snow Creek Saloon in Red Lodge. Near the Meeteetsee Trail bridge over Rock Creek, just south of town, about five miles from where he killed Wolf Number Ten, he passes a sheriff's patrol car so close that he brushes the deputy's arm. The policemen pull him over and direct him to get into the back seat of the patrol car. He asks if he can take a pee first. They say okay. McKittrick plunges into the roadside brush and hightails it for glory.

The officers charge in after him. Owing to the Quarter Beers,

Chad McKittrick wore this t-shirt in the 1995 Fourth of July parade in Red Lodge. At his trial the following February, he testified that he did not know that the animal he had shot was a wolf.

the chase is short. They search his pickup and find marijuana. McKittrick is charged with possession of dangerous drugs, reckless driving, driving under the influence of alcohol, and resisting arrest. He is released on bond.

As summer wanes, McKittrick starts yelling and waving his guns at people whom he considers to be driving too fast past his house. From time to time he is seen shooting randomly into the air, often wearing a black cowboy hat and no shirt. He threatens the life of a neighbor's dog. Federal Express refuses to deliver to anyone in the neighborhood until somebody does something about the madman with the guns and the hat. McKittrick's admirers in the bars—of whom there are more than a few—buy him drink after drink. He gives autographs all around, sometimes offering his signature without being asked.

U.S. Magistrate Richard Anderson rules that McKittrick has violated the principal terms of his release from federal custody, namely, that he not break any federal, state, or local law while awaiting trial. Anderson orders that McKittrick undergo a psychiatric evaluation and then be held in jail while the court studies the report.

October 23, 24, and 25, 1995

Twelve Montana citizens—modest, attentive, clearly unused to being watched so hard—sit in the jury box at the federal district court in Billings, hearing the testimony of Dusty Steinmasel, Tim Eicher, Chad McKittrick, and the government's team of scientific experts. The defendant claims that he thought that Wolf Number Ten was a dog. Steinmasel testifies that McKittrick knew perfectly well that he was shooting a wolf. The jury's deliberation lasts an hour and fifteen minutes.

Chad McKittrick is found guilty of killing a member of a threatened species, guilty of possessing its remains, and guilty of transporting it.

February 22, 1996

Judge Anderson sentences Chad McKittrick to six months' imprisonment, recommending that the time be broken into three months in the Yellowstone County Detention Center and three months in a "pre-release center" in Billings called Alpha House, to be followed by one year of parole during which he must undergo random drug tests and warrantless searches of his house and truck. He is also fined ten thousand dollars, which, being indigent, he cannot pay but for which he will be held responsible should he ever be able to pay it.

"I know now it was a big mistake," says McKittrick to the court.

"All I can say, judge, is that I apologize and that it wasn't my intent to kill a wolf. I thought it was a dog. Also I didn't intend to hit it. I'm sorry for all the trouble."

Still lying.

Consequences

1. Chad McKittrick's case was taken up by several organizations of wolf haters, most notably the Mountain States Legal Foundation, the law firm founded by former Secretary of the Interior James Watt. Throughout 1996, there were repeated attempts to have the conviction reversed or a new trial instituted. All failed.

On January 24, 1997, McKittrick's lawyers appeared before Federal District Court Judge Jack Shanstrom to ask that his conviction and sentence be thrown out on the grounds that McKittrick did not *knowingly* kill a wolf. On February 7, 1997, Shanstrom denied the appeal.

On April 28, 1998, the Ninth Circuit Court of Appeals—presented with a blizzard of technical arguments prepared by a team of highly sophisticated (and highly paid) attorneys—ruled that McKittrick's conviction was valid but that because he had accepted a degree of responsibility for his crime, the case should be remanded to Judge Anderson with a recommendation that the sentence be reduced. The judge cut the term from six months to three.

McKittrick's legal team then filed a petition for a writ of certiorari asking the United States Supreme Court to review the case, but on January 15, 1999, the court declined to hear it. McKittrick's sentence, therefore, stood.

Throughout the more than three years of appeals, he had remained free. On February 17, 1999, Chad McKittrick went to prison for the killing of Wolf Number Ten.

2. Wolf Number Nine, safe, guarded, and fed, back in the old Rose Creek pen, raised her eight pups in peace. For the first months, the pups rarely showed their faces outside the makeshift den that the biologists had built for them. As they grew into big-footed, big-eared, tumbling kids, the pups retained their mother's terror of people. All eight were healthy and strong.

One of Nine and Ten's pups, in June of 1995, seemed to be looking forward to a vaccination with about as much enthusiasm as most other youngsters. Mike Phillips is holding the pup while veterinarian Mark Johnson tries to steady him.

There was one scary moment, on July 29, 1995, when a storm blew down two big Douglas-fir trees that smashed the fence to the ground. None of the wolves were hurt, but all eight pups escaped. Nine herself, ever cautious, stayed home.

The pups were gangly adolescents now, looking more like wolves than puppies, but they were far from ready to venture out on their own. Two returned right away through a hole the trees had torn in the fence, and two more, after that was patched, climbed a slanting trunk and dropped in. Two others were trapped and shoved back inside, and then one of them escaped again. The remaining three were never caught, but they never went far. Every morning they would make shady beds in the aspens nearby, and at evening they would snuffle, whimper, and howl through the chain-link division between

In June of 1995 Number Nine was still nursing all eight pups, as can readily be seen by her swollen teats.

Nine and Ten's pup Number Twenty-three in summer 1995. Having escaped when a tree fell on the pen fence, he was never radio-collared, and he disappeared that December.

Nine and Ten's son Twenty-one would grow up to lead the Druid Pack, which at its peak comprised thirty-seven members. They were infamous for killing other wolves.

Pup Seventeen in summer 1995. She and her three sisters all became mothers the following spring. Theirs were the first native-born Yellowstone wolves in seven decades.

themselves and the rest of the family. One night, one of the three out-side pups somehow managed—a supposedly impossible feat—to climb the fence and get back in.

As autumn turned the valley gold and white, a Crystal Creek yearling designated Eight showed up, tussling in the snow with the two Rose Creek pups who remained outside the pen. He also snuffled and whined and put on something of a romantic display—insofar as that was possible through chain link—for Number Nine.

At the age of seventeen months, Number Eight was not quite an adult and had little to offer by way of knowledge or skill, but come winter he would be able to do the job of an adult male if no other beat him to it. And a green step-uncle for eight always-hungry pups would be, surely, better than none.

Park Superintendent Mike Finley took President Bill Clinton out to the Lamar Valley in August 1995 to show him what was now wolf country—thanks in no small part to Clinton's Interior Department. Chelsea Clinton, at left, and her friend Rebecca Kolsky came along. Nobody saw a wolf that day.

By October 1995 the pups weighted fifty to sixty pounds apiece. Biologists Wayne Brewster, at left, and Doug Smith.

On October 9, 1995, After netting and then radio-collaring the six pups inside the pen, the wolf team shared a pause of silent recognition of what they knew to be a historic moment in the return of the wolf to Yellowstone. Hulking Carter Niemeyer, quiet Mark Johnson, lean and ironic Doug Smith, intense and impatient Mike Phillips looked in on the shed where Number Nine cowered, hiding, hopelessly, from them. The pups were big, rangy, all muscle, ready to hunt. Newcomer Eight and the two pups outside the pen were near, just inside the forest shadows. The men unbolted and removed a panel of the fence and set up their remote-action cameras there.

Within a few hours, Nine and all six pups had left the Rose Creek Pen—right through the gate. By eleven o'clock in the morning they had joined the outside pups and Number Eight on a hillside a mile away.

Nine remained firmly in charge of the pack, and she accepted Eight as her mate, though clearly second in command. He in turn—better by far than a step-uncle—adopted Nine and Ten's pups as his own. That winter, Nine gave birth to three pups sired by Number Eight.

In January 1996, seventeen new wolves arrived from British Columbia, including a pack named for Druid Peak, who quickly showed a propensity for attacking any other wolves they encountered. The Soda Butte pack produced three pups that spring. The Druid Peak pack killed the Crystal Creek alpha male in the early spring before he had a chance to mate, and his pack therefore bore no pups. But Nine's daughter Seven, having paired with ex-Crystal Number Two, also gave birth to three pups. This new pack—the first native-born pack of Yellowstone wolves since their extirpation so long ago—was named for the naturalist Aldo Leopold, who had pleaded through much of his life for the restoration of the wolf to Yellowstone.

Nine and Ten's daughters—Sixteen, Seventeen, Eighteen, and Nineteen—all became mothers themselves. Eighteen eventually contributed thirty-two pups to the fast-growing population. Of Nine and Ten's four sons, only one survived to breeding age. Number Twenty was killed in a bloody battle with the Druids. Number Twenty-two

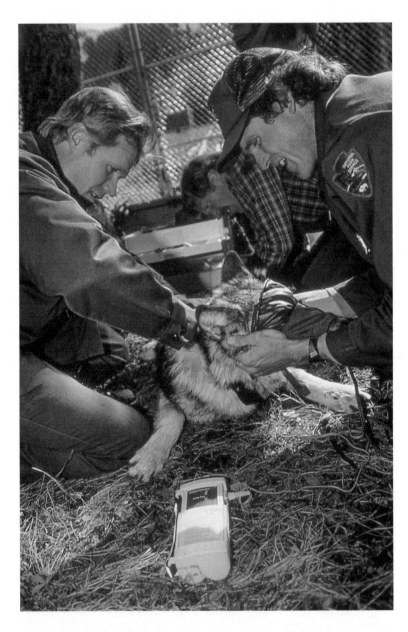

Mike Phillips and Doug Smith radio-collared the six of Nine's eight pups who remained inside the Rose Creek pen, and then they set them free.

lasted less than two months after his release: One December night in 1995, he ran headlong into a UPS truck along the Lamar Valley road. Twenty-three—one of the escapees of the Douglas-fir crash, and therefore never radio-collared—disappeared from the pack in December 1996, and no one ever knew what had happened to him.

Twenty-one, however, more than made up for his brothers' bad luck. He stayed a long time with his mother and his stepfather Number Eight, long enough, in fact, that his first mate was his sister Nineteen, in 1997. Late the same year he invaded and took over the infamous Druids and led them to terrifying dominion. At one point under Twenty-one's leadership the pack had three litters comprising twenty-one pups, and thirty-seven members in all: The Druid Peak pack had become the biggest wolf pack ever known anywhere in the world. Their story remains to be told.

Eight and Nine continued as the alpha pair of the Rose Creek pack, and had pups together again in 1997, 1998, and 1999. Their offspring founded many new packs. By the year 2000, the genes of Wolf Number Nine were present in eighty percent of Yellowstone's wolves.

None of Nine and Eight's pups survived in 2000. Her fur by then was nearly all white. In the spring she seems to have gone alone into the Absaroka-Beartooth Wilderness. Just as when she and Number Ten had headed north five years before, no one could locate her radio signal or find her tracks in the snow. Wolf Number Nine simply disappeared.

3. The wolves today, from the original thirty-one brought to Yellowstone from Canada in 1995 and 1996, now number about five hundred. (The latest official figures are from 2013.) Many of them carry on the DNA of Wolves Nine and Ten. They have long since overflowed the boundaries of the 2.2-million-acre national park and are distributed throughout the twenty million acres of the Greater Yellowstone Ecosystem.

Also in 1995 and 1996, thirty-five wolves were reintroduced to the central Idaho wilderness. The present numbers are disputed, but

Wolf watching has become a major activity in Yellowstone. It contributes hundreds of thousands of dollars a year to local economies.

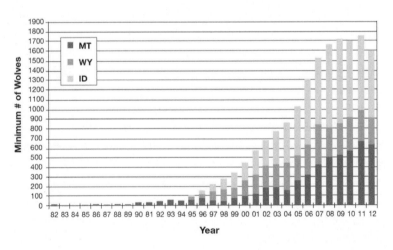

Northern Rocky Mountain Wolf population trends in Montana, Idaho, and Wyoming 1982–2012.

by any estimate there are a lot of wolves in Idaho—at least seven hundred, perhaps as many as nine hundred—and they have begun to col-
onize Washington and Oregon. One Oregon wolf has been visiting
northern California from time to time.

Wolves were already present in small numbers in northern Idaho
and northwestern Montana, and those populations have grown dramatically as well.

The U.S. Fish and Wildlife Service estimates that the Northern
Rocky Mountains are now home to about seventeen hundred wolves.

In short, the restoration of the gray wolf to the American West
has been a spectacular success.

—If only it were so simple. There has been a rising wave of hatred
of the wolf, much of it based in misunderstanding but nonetheless
fierce. Livestock interests always opposed the reintroduction, and the
wolf's advocates crafted a restoration plan that provided for the killing
of wolves that preyed on livestock and the compensation of ranchers
who lost stock to wolves. In the event, there has been amazingly little
depredation, but that hasn't prevented politicians and scaremongers
from convincing many residents of the region that the livestock indus-
try's very viability is in danger. Many hunters have come to believe
that wolves are destroying elk and deer herds.

It is certainly true that some wolves have killed some livestock.
Livestock owners have only rarely been able to catch them in the act
and kill those wolves legally. Government agents have been quite suc-
cessful, however, in taking out not only individual guilty wolves but
sometimes whole packs. There are now wolf hunting and trapping
seasons in Idaho, Montana, and Wyoming—long seasons, with generous limits—which have curbed wolf population growth and thereby
reduced the depredation risk which would otherwise have increased
as wolves began to spread farther out from the wild areas where they
now mostly live. Yet there are still plenty of wolves with easy access
to cows and calves and sheep and lambs—easy pickings that they just
don't take.

This was what the biologists predicted all along, and few were the non-scientists who believed them. Here are the facts.

There are about 2,600,000 cows and calves in the state of Montana. In 2013, somewhere between forty-five and fifty-eight of them were killed by wolves. If we take the larger number, we can calculate that 0.000022 of the cattle population was lost to wolf depredation, or 2.2 thousandths of one percent. In 2012, of Montana's 230,000 sheep, 4,300 were killed by disease, 6,000 by birth complications, 2,700 by old age, 900 by poison, 5,600 by weather, and 200 by falling and not being able to get up. Predator killings included 800 by bears, 13,900 by coyotes, 900 by dogs, 400 by eagles, 600 by foxes, 700 by mountain lions, 100 by "other animals," and 600 by unidentified predators. Three hundred sheep were killed by wolves. That's 0.0013.

The United States Department of Agriculture supplies us with this handy pie chart that makes the numbers a little easier to grasp:

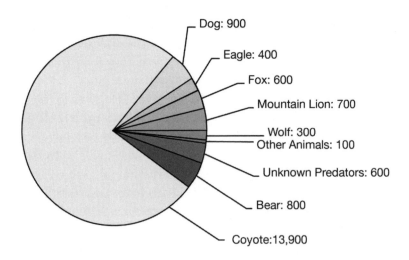

Sheep and lamb loss by predators, 2012.

In Wyoming in 2011, of the state's 1,300,000 cattle, thirty-five were killed by wolves—2.6 thousandths of a percent. In Idaho in 2012, where the state's official wolf count was just under seven hundred and the cattle population 2,200,000, ninety-two cows and calves were killed, or 4.1 thousandths of one percent.

Now, if one of those cows is yours, it's a serious loss. A young, productive mother cow and her expected lifetime progeny can be worth several thousand dollars, perhaps the difference between profit and loss in the precarious economy of ranching. Compensation for losses to wolf predation, however, has been provided from the beginning—at first by the conservation group Defenders of Wildlife and more recently by the states, backed up with federal money. It covers only the market value of the animal, though, not her future productivity. But nobody pays ranchers a nickel when their cattle or sheep die of disease, freeze to death, fall off cliffs, or get eaten by bears. And stockmen have learned to live with those losses for generations. There's something unique about the ravening wolf, something inexplicable, mythic, seated deep in the Western soul.

Some hunters believe that wolves are competing with them for the same prey, but in fact wolves for the most part kill animals the hunters don't want—the young, the lame, the sick, and the old. Hunters want either trophies—big bull elk or buck deer with big antlers—or big healthy females with lots of tender meat for the family freezer. All too many hunters in wolf country have come to believe that wolves are *wiping out* their prey populations. It's generally useless to point out that a predator that exterminated its prey population would be exterminating itself. You'll be laughed (or thrown) out of the bar.

Try the scientific arguments, then, that predation has literally modeled both predators and prey in every ecosystem on earth, that the wolf and the elk have co-evolved through millennia, that the apex predator—which is what the wolf is—is in fact essential to the functioning of a healthy food web, all the way down to the microorganisms in the soil. This will brand you as a member of the "fact-based community," and if, as is likely, your interlocutor is a member of the "faith-based community," no amount of mere fact is going to get you anywhere.

What has so often happened since the return of the wolf is that a man who has hunted elk in the same area for years has found, increasingly, that he's going home empty-handed, convinced that the wolves have killed off all the elk. The usual case is that the elk that used to gather in herds out in the open are hiding in small groups back in the trees. The wolf pack, unlike the hunter, can smell them, can chase them and identify the vulnerable individuals, and, with luck, kill a week's worth of groceries. (Even with their puny prey, wolves succeed in the hunt remarkably seldom. Elk are very good at getting away or fighting back.)

Elk numbers have in fact fallen in some places where wolves are abundant, and it is natural that people blame the wolves. Sometimes wolves have played a significant role in those declines. Sometimes they haven't. Here's an example.

In recent years the whitebark pine tree, whose nuts have historically been the richest source of calories for Yellowstone's grizzly bears, has been hit by a double blow—an infestation of mountain pine beetles and the deadly white pine blister rust. That food supply for the bears, therefore, has all but disappeared. At the same time, somebody dumped non-native lake trout into Yellowstone Lake, until then home to a pristine population of cutthroat trout. Lake trout are much larger than cutthroats, and they immediately began gobbling up the young cuts by the thousands. Cutthroats spawn in the streams that feed the lake, and from time immemorial, in late spring grizzlies would snatch them out and feed on them almost exclusively for as long as a month—and now the cutthroat were gone as well. But grizzlies are smart and adaptable. It happens that the collapsed cutthroat spawning season coincides with the time when elk calves are young and vulnerable, and before long the bears were hauling down young elk in impressive numbers. They also got quite good at stealing kills from wolves. Add in some deep-snow winters—which impede elk movement but don't bother wolves in the least—and down comes the Northern Range elk population.

Years pass. Things change. By February 2013, in the valley where I used to live (I was a partner in a cattle ranch), the local paper, the

Big Timber *Pioneer*, under the headline LANDOWNERS ASK FOR MORE ELK CONTROL, reports that "Elk populations have increased dramatically over the past six to eight years. . . . [In] District 560 (includes all forks of the Boulder River) the elk population grew 100 percent between 2008 and 2013." Too many elk! And during that time, at least one wolf pack resided there year-round.

I now spend part of every summer just north of Big Timber, and I've never met nicer, finer people in my life than the people there. But except among my conservationist friends, I know to refrain from talking about wolves regarding either livestock or game, indeed wolves at all, because you just don't know if you'll have lit a short fuse to a keg of dynamite.

There is a whole culture in the United States—a growing one, it seems—that consciously walls out facts it doesn't want to know. These facts cluster together: evolution by natural selection; climate change; our society's growing recognition of equal rights for all persons; the citizen's responsibilities to the citizenry; the damage humans have done to natural systems and our duty to try to heal them.

Today's wars against the wolf go well beyond denial of fact, however. In a civilization sufficiently advanced, bless us all, that lynchings are no longer possible, savage joy can still be taken in wolf slaughter. In late December 2013, Salmon, Idaho, held a "Youth Predator Derby" with $1,000 prizes and trophies for kids who killed the biggest wolf and the most coyotes, with special awards in the 10–11 and 12–14 age categories. Also in Idaho, a former Republican candidate for governor, Rex Rammell, tried to organize wolf-killing parties to use helicopters, aerial gunners, hunters, trapping, snaring, and poison. Lest Rammell be considered an outlier, the actual governor of Idaho, Butch Otter, recently passed a bill declaring the presence of the gray wolf "a disaster emergency," and in addition to the state's already generous hunting and trapping season there soon began a campaign of gunning down whole packs in areas where elk populations were deemed to have declined. For one wilderness area the state hired a professional hunter to kill two packs of wolves. Facebook and Twitter teem with photographs of dead, dying, trapped, and maimed wolves, with the perpetrators grinning proudly alongside. Wolf-hatred organizations proliferate. Formerly virtuous organizations—the Rocky Mountain Elk Foundation is one—become delusional on the subject of wolves. Idaho now allows wolf hunting somewhere in the state 365 days a year, with up to five wolves per hunter, five per trapper. The Montana Department of Fish, Wildlife and Parks continues to press for increased hunting and trapping.

Why?

A recent study at Montana State University concludes that "Using the current data available, wolves are not having a significant effect on elk harvest in Montana." The study also says, however, that the sale of hunting licenses had declined quite drastically, and therefore the number of elk reported killed by hunters had also declined—perhaps a partial explanation for the widespread belief in elk decline.[1]

The U.S. Fish and Wildlife Service has tried repeatedly to lift all federal protection from the wolves of the Northern Rockies—not that you'd notice that they're so well protected to start with. The latest proposal for removing the wolf from the list of threatened species was based almost entirely on a single analysis, which, an independent scientific review panel concluded, in the affectless voice of doom, "does not currently represent the 'best available science.'"[2] Translated into English, that means, "Go back and finish your homework." Presumably, now, months if not years more of bureaucratic and legal tumult are still to come.

The restoration of the wolf to Yellowstone was the bravest and finest event in Yellowstone's history, but it was much more: It was an act of immense symbolic significance, an example of how powerful doing the right thing can be.

It has turned out not to be so easy to establish its biological significance, however, and it is on that that many wolf advocates have

[1] Steven Robert Hazen. The Impact of Wolves on Elk Hunting in Montana. M.S. in applied economics thesis. Montana State University, 2012.

[2] Review of proposed rule regarding status of the wolf under the Endangered Species Act. National Center for Ecological Analysis and Synthesis, University of California, Santa Barbara, January 2014.

relied to justify the millions of dollars spent, the battles, the heartache, above all the absolute *rightness* of bringing back the wolf, this great act of healing. The prevailing story has been a romantic one, of what is known as a trophic cascade, in which the reintroduction of the wolf causes changes that "cascade" throughout the ecosystem, making everything better and better. It goes like this:

The redistribution of elk, frightened away from the waterways by wolves, contributes to the recovery of streamside willows. Willow regeneration increases nesting habitat for songbirds, stabilizes bank vegetation and thereby slows erosion, and brings back the beaver from its near-disappearance. The beaver's dams create ponds that provide new habitat for fish, for the otters that prey on the fish, for the muskrats that eat the newly revitalized vegetation, for amphibians and reptiles that exploit the new habitat, and for ducks, geese, swans, and shorebirds. The trophic cascade story also prominently features the recovery of aspen—which was believed to have been nibbled to mere sprouts by elk. Healthier aspen groves mean better songbird habitat. Shrubs under the aspen canopy produce larger berry crops— food for bears and birds.

Wolves *have* reduced Yellowstone Park's coyote population significantly, that much is certain. One early estimate put the decline at forty percent, though there may have been some recovery since then. In any case such a change is bound to have significant effects, although they're very hard to pin down specifically. For example, the trophic cascade story would predict a rise in foxes due to increased availability of rabbits, ground squirrels, voles, mice, and other small mammals. In fact, foxes were rarely seen on the Northern Range before 1995, and says biologist Rolf Peterson, they "are now not uncommon." But that change, he warns, could be due to a reduction of direct suppression by coyotes (coyotes are tough on foxes just as wolves are on coyotes), or to the increased prey base. "No one," says Peterson, "can say." The increase in small mammals ought to be good news for hawks, owls, weasels, and badgers as well, and theoretically, the decrease in coyotes would also increase the availability of snow-shoe hares, the primary prey of the rare (and declining) lynx—but none of those effects have been measured either.

The leftovers from wolf kills are scavenged by ravens, eagles, black bears, grizzlies, and countless species of insects that are fed on by countless species of other small creatures. All that has been commonly observed, but again, the precise effects remain to be documented.

Bank stabilization—if it's happening—narrows the creeks and rivers, deepening the pools and agitating and thereby oxygenating the riffles, hence increasing the production of the insects and other invertebrates that fish feed on, while also improving shelter and spawning habitat for the fish. Growing fish populations mean more prey for ospreys, eagles, pelicans, mink, and grizzlies.

And so on and so on, till you have a wholly invigorated ecosystem, a more fertile range—more grass, more wildflowers and other soft-stemmed plants, more-vigorous shrubs, better nutrition for elk and deer. More food for wolves.

—If only it were so simple. A new analysis by the renowned wolf expert Rolf Peterson and colleagues including Yellowstone project leader Doug Smith[3] demonstrates that the wolf's role in the decline of the elk population of Yellowstone's Northern Range has been much less than is commonly believed. With that fact alone the simple trophic cascade becomes a mud puddle. Drought and hunting by humans were huge factors in the first decade after wolf reintroduction. In the years immediately following the wolf introduction—when it was widely thought that there were "too many" elk on the Northern Range—the state of Montana maintained a late-season elk hunt, which drew some of the region's rather less sporting sportsmen to array themselves scant yards from the park border to greet the elk as they made their way along their traditional migration path to the north. To aid in rapid reduction of the herd, cow elk were included. At that time of the year, they were pregnant. Several years of drought didn't help. As the elk population sank, fast, Montana closed the season. The sportsmen were outraged, and blamed the wolves.

---

[3] Rolf O. Peterson, John A. Vucetich, Joseph M. Bump, and Douglas W. Smith. Trophic cascades in a multi-causal world: Isle Royale and Yellowstone. *Annual Review of Ecology, Evolution, and Systematics*, 2014 (in press).

By the late 1990s, the grizzly bear population on the Northern Range had tripled. Between 2003 and 2005, annual elk calf mortality was estimated at 78 percent, and bears (both grizzly and black) accounted for between 58 and 60 percent of those killings, whereas wolves were responsible for only 14 to 17 percent. Since 2005, wolves have been killing more elk, but that is too recent for large-scale ecosystem effects to have appeared.

The observed effects on aspen turn out to have been spotty, and may have other contributing factors besides overbrowsing by elk. The recovery of willow may have more to do with changes in the water table, or lack of beavers, or just precipitation, than with changes in elk behavior. The authors continue knocking down similar assumptions like ninepins. They don't address climate change, but there is no question that it is already having strong effects—winters in the Lamar are growing decidedly warmer and shorter—and it will doubtless have unpredictable destabilizing effects in coming years. Peterson and his co-authors conclude, "A trophic cascade . . . is an intellectual construct born in an imaginary world of simple food chains governed by equilibrium dynamics. That is not the world in which we live."

They offer in its place a deeper justification for conservation not only of the wolf but of all carnivores, one put forward by the great wolf biologist Durward Allen in 1954:

> Impartial sympathy toward all creatures, regardless of their diet, is an attitude of the cultivated mind. It is a measure of man's civilization. If ever we are to achieve a reasonable concord with the earth on which we live, it will be by our willingness to recognize [and] tolerate . . . the biological forces and relationships both in our own numbers and in the living things about us.[4]

---

[4] *Our Wildlife Legacy.* New York: Funk and Wagnalls Company, 1954, 256-57.

The return of the wolf to Yellowstone has vast historical meaning. It will require a last moment's digression to explain that.

In conservation, every victory has been a battle won in a war we believe that we ultimately lose. This, the Anthropocene Era (when human influence dominates the global ecosystem), we're told, is the Age of Extinction. The United Nations Population Programme is now projecting that within less than a hundred years the surface of our planet may be crowded with as many as ten billion people. Add the inevitable acceleration of the carbon dioxide burden in the atmosphere, a global water crisis, insufficient agricultural land, and you have not only mass extinctions but all sorts of ecosystem collapse.

But the U.N. also states that in populations where three factors emerge among women, things change radically.[5] When girls learn to read and write, when women have political freedom, and when women control their own money, the birth rate falls to replacement rate or lower. This has already happened in most of the "first world"— North America, Europe, Japan, Australia, and so forth. And female literacy, political freedom, and economic autonomy in many of the less-developed countries are growing fast. It may just be that by the year 2100, although the world population will still be huge, for the first time in history it will begin to decline.

What that can mean is that wherever we are able to conserve the great treasures of human civilization, they will still be there for the new world. The people of the twenty-second century need not be wandering in a wasteland. Imagine that Notre Dame still stands at the heart of Paris. Imagine that the Prado and the Uffizi and the Metropolitan still house their magnificent art. Imagine that half-ton bluefin tuna still race across the Atlantic to spawn in the Mediterranean Sea. Imagine lions still pursuing the great herds of wildebeest across the Serengeti.

Believe that the largest essentially intact wild ecosystem in the temperate zones of the earth—Greater Yellowstone—will survive.

[5] United Nations Economic and Social Council, Department of Public Information, Commission on Population and Development, 2011.

Believe that the grizzly bears and bison and elk and wolves of Yellow-stone will still interact as they have done through all the ages of their co-evolution. That is what Nine and Ten will have given us.

That is what those who brought the wolf back to Yellowstone—who didn't just conserve something almost lost, but restored something that really was lost—that is what they will have left to the future.

BIBLIOGRAPHY

*For readers interested in pursuing the story of the
return of the wolf to Yellowstone in greater depth,
I have marked certain entries with an asterisk.*

—*T.M.*

Allen, Durward L. *Our Wildlife Legacy.* New York: Funk and Wagnalls
Company, 1954.

_____. *Wolves of Minong: Their Vital Role in a Wild Commu-
nity.* Boston: Houghton Mifflin, 1979.

*Askins, Renée. *Shadow Mountain: A Memoir of Wolves, a Woman,
and the Wild.* New York: Doubleday, 2002. A highly personal memoir
by the founder of the Wolf Fund and one of the most effective advocates in bringing the wolf back to Yellowstone.

Barker, Rocky. *Saving All the Parts: Reconciling Economics and the
Endangered Species Act.* Washington, DC: Island Press, 1993.

Berger, Joel. Greater Yellowstone's native ungulates: myths and
realities. *Conservation Biology,* September 1991.

Brewster, Wayne G., Norman A. Bishop, Paul Schullery, and John
Varley. The public has spoken: wolves belong in Yellowstone. *International Wolf,* summer 1995.

Clark, Tim W., Elizabeth Dawn Amato, Donald G. Whittemore, and
Ann H. Harvey. Policy and programs for ecosystem management in

the Greater Yellowstone Ecosystem: an analysis. *Conservation Biology*, September 1991.

Consolo Murphy, S. and D.W. Smith. Documenting trends in Yellowstone's beaver population: a comparison of aerial and ground surveys in the Yellowstone Lake Basin. In R.J. Anderson and D. Harmon, eds. *Yellowstone Lake: Hotbed of Chaos or Reservoir of Resilience? Proceedings of the Sixth Biennial Scientific Conference on the Greater Yellowstone Ecosystem.* Yellowstone National Park, WY: National Park Service, Yellowstone Center for Resources and Hancock, MI: The George Wright Society, 2002.

Curlee, A. Peyton, Anne-Marie Gillesberg, and Denise Casey, eds. *Greater Yellowstone Predators: Ecology and Conservation in a Changing Landscape—Proceedings of the Third Biennial Conference of the Greater Yellowstone Ecosystem.* Jackson, WY: Northern Rockies Conservation Cooperative, 1995.

Eberhardt, L.L., R.A. Garrott, D.W. Smith, P.J. White, and R.O. Peterson. Assessing the impact of wolves on ungulate prey. *Ecological Applications*, 2003.

*Ferguson, Gary. *The Yellowstone Wolves: The First Year.* Helena, MT: Falcon Press, 1996.

*Fischer, Hank. *Wolf Wars: The Remarkable Inside Story of the Restoration of Wolves to Yellowstone.* Helena, MT: Falcon Press, 1995. The best account of the political struggle leading up to the reintroduction, by one of its leading advocates.

Forester, J.D., A.R. Ives, M.G. Turner, D.P. Anderson, D. Fortin, H.L. Beyer, D.W. Smith, and M.S. Boyce. State-space models link elk movement patterns to landscape characteristics in Yellowstone National Park. *Ecological Monographs* 77, 2007.

Fortin, D., H.L. Beyer, M.S. Boyce, D.W. Smith, T. Duchesne, J.S. Mao. Wolves influence elk movements: behavior shapes a trophic cascade in Yellowstone National Park. *Ecology* 86, 2005.

Fritts, Steven H. "Soft" and "hard" release: planning the reintroduction. *International Wolf,* summer 1995.

Fritts, Steven H., Edward E. Bangs, and James F. Gore. The relationship of wolf recovery to habitat conservation and biodiversity in the northwestern United States. *Landscape and Urban Planning* 28, 1994.

Haber, Gordon C. Biological, conservation, and ethical implications of exploiting and controlling wolves. *Conservation Biology,* August 1996.

Haines, Aubrey L. *The Yellowstone Story: A History of Our First National Park.* Yellowstone National Park, WY: Yellowstone Museum and Library Association, 1977.

Halfpenny, James C. *Charting Yellowstone's Wolves: A Record of Wolf Restoration.* Gardiner, MT: A Naturalist's World, 2012.

Halfpenny, James. C., and Diann Thompson. *Discovering Yellowstone Wolves: Watcher's Guide.* Gardiner, MT: A Naturalist's World, 1996.

Hanauska-Brown, L., L. Bradley, J. Gude, N. Lance, K. Laudon, A. Messer, A. Nelson, M. Ross, and J. Steuber. *Montana Gray Wolf Conservation and Management 2011 Annual Report.* Helena, MT: Montana Department of Fish, Wildlife & Parks, 2011.

Hazen, Steven Robert. The impact of wolves on elk hunting in Montana. M.S. in applied economics thesis, Montana State University, 2012.

Jobes, Patrick C. The Greater Yellowstone social system. *Conservation Biology,* September 1991.

Kauffman, M.J., N. Varley, D.W. Smith, D.R. Stahler, D.R. Mac-Nulty, and M.S. Boyce. Landscape heterogeneity shapes predation in a newly restored predator-prey system. *Ecology Letters* 10, 2007.

*Keiter, Robert B, and Mark S. Boyce, eds. *The Greater Yellowstone Ecosystem: People and Nature on America's Wildlands.* New Haven: Yale University Press, 1991. An invaluable overview.

Keiter, Robert B., and Patrick T. Holscher. Wolf recovery under the Endangered Species Act: a study in contemporary federalism. *Public Land Law Review* 11, 1990.

Keiter, Robert B., and Harvey Locke. Law and large carnivore conservation in the Rocky Mountains of the U.S. and Canada. *Conservation Biology*, August 1996.

*Lowry, William R. *Repairing Paradise: The Restoration of Nature in America's National Parks.* Washington, DC: Brookings Institution Press, 2009. An excellent exploration of the philosophy of *why*.

*Lyon, Ted B., and Will N. Graves, with contributions by others. *The Real Wolf: The Science, Politics, and Economics of Co-existing with Wolves in Modern Times.* Ted B. Lyon, 2014. Absolute bilge—a valuable example, nonetheless, of the kind of "evidence" amassed against the wolf by its antagonists.

Mao, J.S., M.S. Boyce, D.W. Smith, F.J. Singer, D.J. Vales, J.M. Vore and E.M. Merrill. Habitat selection by elk before and after wolf reintroduction in Yellowstone National Park. *Journal of Wildlife Management* 69 (4), 2005.

*McNamee, Thomas. *The Return of the Wolf to Yellowstone.* New York: Henry Holt, 1997.

_____. Yellowstone's missing element. *Audubon*, January 1986.

_____. Yellowstone's missing wolves. *Defenders*, November–December 1992.

Mech, L.D., D.W. Smith, K.M. Murphy, and D.R. MacNulty. Winter severity and wolf predation on a formerly wolf-free elk herd. *Journal of Wildlife Management* 65, 2001.

_____. The challenge and opportunity of recovering wolf populations. *Conservation Biology,* April 1995.

_____. Updating our thinking on the role of human activity in wolf recovery. U.S. Fish and Wildlife Service Information Bulletin, 1993.

_____. *The Way of the Wolf.* Stillwater, MN: Voyageur Press, 1991.

*_____. *The Wolf: The Ecology and Behavior of an Endangered Species.* New York: Doubleday, 1970, and Minneapolis: University of Minnesota Press, 1981. Still the definitive text on the gray wolf by the leading expert in the world.

*_____, and Luigi Boitani, eds. *Wolves: Behavior, Ecology, and Conservation.* Chicago and London: University of Chicago Press, 2003. Technical, but the state of the art in scientific understanding of wolf biology and behavior.

Merkle, J.A., D.R. Stahler, and D.W. Smith. Interference competition between gray wolves and coyotes in Yellowstone National Park. *Canadian Journal of Zoology/Revue Canadienne De Zoologie* 87, 2009.

Metz, Matthew C., John A. Vucetich, Douglas W. Smith, Daniel R. Stahler, and Rolf O. Peterson. Effect of sociality and season on gray wolf (*Canis lupus*) foraging behavior: implications for estimating summer kill rate. *PLOS ONE*, March 1, 2011.

Metz, M.C., D.W. Smith, J.A. Vucetich, D.R. Stahler, and R.O. Peterson. Seasonal patterns of predation for gray wolves in the multi-prey system of Yellowstone National Park. *Journal of Animal Ecology* doi: 10.1111/j.1365-2656.2011.01945.x, 2012.

National Center for Ecological Analysis and Synthesis, University of California, Santa Barbara. Review of proposed rule regarding status of the wolf under the Endangered Species Act, January 2014.

Niemeyer, Carter. Precapture operation—snaring and radio-collaring of "Judas" wolves. *International Wolf*, summer 1995.

*_____. *Wolfer: A Memoir*. Boise, ID: Bottlefly Press, 2010. A dramatic first-person account by a former predator control agent who became the wolf project's lead trapper and a fierce conservationist.

Oakleaf, J.K., D.L. Murray, J.R. Oakleaf, E.E. Bangs, C.M. Mack, D.W. Smith, J.A. Fontaine, M.D. Jimenez, T.J. Meier, and C.C. Niemeyer. Habitat selection by recolonizing wolves in the Northern Rocky Mountains of the United States. *Journal of Wildlife Management* 70, 2006.

Packard, Jane M., L. David Mech, and Ulysses S. Seal. Social influences on reproduction in wolves. In Ludwig N. Carbyn, ed., *Wolves in Canada: Their Status, Biology, and Management*. Edmonton: Canadian Wildlife Service Report Series No. 45, 1983.

Packard, Jane M., Ulysses S. Seal, L. David Mech, and Edward D. Plotka. Causes of reproductive failure in two family groups of wolves (*Canis lupus*). University of Minnesota, Veterans Administration Medical Center, Patuxent Wildlife Research Center, and Marshfield Medical Foundation. *Zeitschrift fur Tierpsychologie* 68,1985.

Peterson, Rolf O., John A. Vucetich, Joseph M. Bump, and Douglas W. Smith. Trophic cascades in a multi-causal world: Isle Royale and Yellowstone. In *Annual Review of Ecology, Evolution, and Systematics,* 2014 (in press).

*Phillips, M. and D.W. Smith. *The Wolves of Yellowstone.* Stillwater, MN: Voyageur Press, 1996. A first-person account of the wolf restoration by the two leaders of the project.

Power, Thomas Michael. Ecosystem preservation and the economy in the Greater Yellowstone area. *Conservation Biology,* September 1991.

Ripple, W.J., E.J. Larsen, R.A. Renkin, and D.W. Smith. Trophic cascades among wolves, elk and aspen on Yellowstone National Park's northern range. *Biological Conservation* 102, 2001.

Ruth, T.K., D.W. Smith, M.A. Haroldson, P.C. Buotte, C.C. Schwartz, H.B. Quigley, S. Cherry, K.M. Murphy, D. Tyers and K. Frey. Large-carnivore response to recreational big-game hunting along the Yellowstone National Park and Absaroka-Beartooth Wilderness boundary. *Wildlife Society Bulletin* 31, 2003.

*Schullery, Paul, ed. *The Yellowstone Wolf: A Guide and Sourcebook.* Norman, OK: University of Oklahoma Press, 1996. Very good on Yellowstone history, the legal issues, and a long view of the future.

*Singer, Francis J., ed. *Grazing Influences on Yellowstone's Northern Range.* Yellowstone National Park, WY, 1990. Technical, and available possibly only in the park's library, but if you really want to get to the bottom of the mysteries of the interaction of elk, bison, and their food, this is the place to go.

Smith, Douglas, and Gary Peterson. *Decade of the Wolf: Returning the Wild to Yellowstone.* Guilford, CT: Lyons Press, 2005.

Smith, Douglas W. Adjusting to new sights, smells and sounds—in captivity. *International Wolf*, summer 1995.

_____. The founder wolves. *International Wolf*, summer 1995.

Smith, D., W. Brewster, and E. Bangs. Wolves in the Greater Yellowstone Ecosystem: restoration of a top carnivore in a complex management environment. In Clark, T., A.P. Curlee, S. Minta, and P. Kareiva, eds., *Carnivores in Ecosystems: The Yellowstone Experience*. New Haven and London: Yale University Press, 1999.

Smith, D.W., T.D. Drummer, K.M. Murphy, D.S. Guernsey, and S.B. Evans. Winter prey selection and estimation of wolf kill rates in Yellowstone National Park, 1995–2000. *Journal of Wildlife Management* 68, 2004.

Smith, D.W., R.O. Peterson, and D. Houston. Yellowstone after wolves. *BioScience* 53, 2003.

Smith, D.W., K.M. Murphy, and S. Monger. Killing of a bison (*Bison bison*) calf, by a wolf (*Canis lupus*), and four coyotes (*Canis latrans*) in Yellowstone National Park. *Canadian Field-Naturalist* 115, 2001.

Smith, D.W., E.E. Bangs, J.K. Oakleaf, C. Mack, J. Fontaine, D. Boyd, M. Jimenez, D.H. Pletscher, C.C. Niemeyer, T.J. Meier, D.R. Stahler, J. Holyan, V.J. Asher, and D.L. Murray. Survival of colonizing wolves in the Northern Rocky Mountains of the United States, 1982–2004. *Journal of Wildlife Management* 74, 2010.

Tucker, Pat, and Daniel H. Pletscher. Attitudes of hunters and residents toward wolves in northwestern Montana. *Wildlife Society Bulletin* 17, 1989.

United States Department of Agriculture, National Agricultural Statistics Service, Montana Sheep and Lamb Loss, 2012.

*United States Department of the Interior, Fish and Wildlife Service. *The Reintroduction of Gray Wolves to Yellowstone National Park and Central Idaho: Final Environmental Impact Statement.* 1994. All the original rules and considerations that went into making the whole thing possible.

*United States Fish and Wildlife Service. Agency review draft, revised Northern Rocky Mountain Wolf Recovery Plan, 1984. No need to read the thing, just look at the date.

_____. Rocky Mountain Wolf Recovery 2012 Interagency Annual Report.

Vucetich, J.A., D.W. Smith, and D.R. Stahler. Influence of harvest, climate, and wolf predation on Yellowstone elk, 1961–2004. *Oikos* 111, 2005.

*Weaver, John L. *The Wolves of Yellowstone.* Washington, DC: U.S. Department of the Interior, Natural Resources Report No. 14, 1978. A document of great historical significance. The reintroduction had been delayed for years by claims that there existed a secretive, remnant population of Yellowstone wolves. Weaver proved definitively that were no wolves in Yellowstone, and opened the way to their restoration a mere seventeen years later.

*Weise, Thomas F., William L. Robinson, Richard A. Hook, and L. David Mech. An experimental translocation of the eastern timber wolf. Twin Cities, MN: U.S. Fish and Wildlife Service, 1975. A fascinating, cautionary account of an earlier attempt at moving and re-establishing wolves. It was a total flop.

Welsch, Jeff. Wolves: A howling success, celebrating 15 years of restoration. *Greater Yellowstone Advocate*, spring 2010.

_____. Changing behavior patterns: presence of wolves keeps

elk on the move, but populations and hunter-success rates remain high. *Greater Yellowstone Advocate*, spring 2010.

Wilmers, C.C., R.L. Crabtree, D.W. Smith, K.M. Murphy, and W.M. Getz. Trophic facilitation by introduced top predators: grey wolf subsidies to scavengers in Yellowstone National Park. *Journal of Animal Ecology* 72, 2003.

Wright, G.J., R.O. Peterson, D.W. Smith, and T.O. Lemke. Selection of northern Yellowstone elk by gray wolves and hunters. *Journal of Wildlife Management* 70, 2006.

*Yellowstone National Park. *Wolves for Yellowstone?* Two-volume report to the U.S. Congress, 1990 and 1992. Hundreds of pages of indispensable *raison d'être*.

ACKNOWLEDGMENTS

The restoration of the gray wolf to Yellowstone was an epic with scores of heroes, dating back to the first advocate of reintroduction, the naturalist Aldo Leopold, in 1944. It would be full fifty years before the biologist Mike Phillips would lead the team that brought living wolves to their ancestral home, and in those decades the complexity of the story and the valor of the actors in it exceed any one writer's capacity to record or even adequately to praise. Here I must confine my humble thanks to those who in the last glorious moments of struggle and victory made time for me in my efforts, first, in my book *The Return of the Wolf to Yellowstone*, to portray this greatest event in the life of Yellowstone National Park and, now, in *The Killing of Wolf Number Ten*, to distill an essence of it.

I must single out Doug Smith, who was second in charge of the wolf project at its beginning and now leads it. Besides his wise and patient counsel to me, Doug has spent countless hours talking to schoolchildren, civic groups, journalists, every audience he can find who need to learn the truth of wolves in this world of misinformation. He has also written for magazines and newspapers, done radio interviews, and appeared on TV. And somehow, meanwhile, he has been conducting outstanding technical research and publishing its results in a wide range of scientific journals. I cannot imagine a finer example of that most necessary of citizens, the scientist unafraid to be an advocate.

There are a number of others who have been remarkably generous with their time and understanding. To the project leader Mike Phillips; to David Mech of the U.S. Fish and Wildlife Service, the world's most knowledgeable authority on the wolf; to the veterinarian Mark Johnson, who never left the wolves from the moment of their capture to their release; to the trapper and tracker supreme Carter Niemeyer; to the strategician Ed Bangs; to their FWS colleague Joe Fontaine, who found Nine and her pups; and to the nonpareil investigator Tim Eicher, I extend heartfelt gratitude. To all the con-servationists who worked so hard through so many years and finally triumphed, especially to my personal heroes Renée Askins of The Wolf Fund, Tom France of the National Wildlife Federation, and Hank Fischer of Defenders of Wildlife, let me speak for the millions who owe you gratitude. To Bill Strachan, who published *The Return of the Wolf to Yellowstone* in 1997 and who now has shepherded this little book to Yellowstone, to David Wilk, who figured out how to publish it in a uniquely creative way, and to David McCormick, my literary agent and friend, my gratitude.

And let a bright spotlight shine on Sandra Nykerk, who spent I can't even think how many hours bringing hopelessly fuzzy and con-trastless photographs to life, and who has been the sweetest and truest of friends. Sandy, you have not only my gratitude but my lifelong affection.

Last, because most, to my dear Elizabeth, my gratitude and all my love.